Margery Kempe

European University Studies

Europäische Hochschulschriften
Publications Universitaires Européennes

Series XIV
Anglo-Saxon Language and Literature

Reihe XIV Série XIV
Angelsächsische Sprache und Literatur
Langue et littérature anglo-saxonnes

Vol./Band 278

PETER LANG
Berne · Berlin · Frankfurt/M. · New York · Paris · Wien

Verena E. Neuburger

Margery Kempe

A Study in Early English Feminism

PETER LANG
Berne · Berlin · Frankfurt/M. · New York · Paris · Wien

Die Deutsche Bibliothek – CIP-Einheitsaufnahme

Neuburger, Verena E.:
Margery Kempe : a study in early English feminism / Verena E.
Neuburger. - Bern ; Berlin ; Frankfurt a.M. ; New York ; Paris ;
Wien : Lang, 1994
 (European university studies : Ser. 14, Anglo-Saxon language and
literature ; Vol. 278)
Zugl.: Zürich, Univ., Diss.
ISBN 3-906752-65-8
NE: Europäische Hochschulschriften / 14

Die vorliegende Arbeit wurde von der Philosophischen Fakultät I
der Universität Zürich im Wintersemester 1993/94 auf Antrag von
Herrn Prof. Dr. H. Petter als Dissertation angenommen.

© Peter Lang, Inc., European Academic Publishers, Berne 1994

All rights reserved.
Reprint or reproduction, even partially, in all forms such as
microfilm, xerography, microfiche, microcard, offset strictly prohibited.

Printed in Germany

TABLE OF CONTENTS

I	INTRODUCTION	7

II	JULIAN OF NORWICH	

a)	Introduction	11
b)	The Life and Visions of Julian of Norwich	13
c)	The Text of Julian of Norwich's *Revelations of Divine Love*	22
d)	Julian of Norwich's Processing of the Visions	25
e)	Julian of Norwich's Teachings	38
	(i) Alle schalle be wele	38
	(ii) I it am	39
	(iii) The Scale of God's Love: the Hazelnut	40
	(iv) Motherhood in God, the Father; God, the Son; and God, the Holy Ghost	41
	(v) Felix Culpa - The Grace of Sin	43
	(vi) Her Lasting Message	44

III	MYSTICISM	47

IV	MARGERY KEMPE	

a)	Textual History	51
b)	Margery Kempe "*p*is creatur"	52
c)	The *Book* and Margery Kempe	57
	(i) The *Book* as Literature	58
	(ii) The *Book* as Biography	63
	(iii) Margery Kempe's Story in Developmental Sequence	66
	(iv) Experience Mirrored in Margery Kempe's *Book*	86
	(v) Why She Wrote	91

V	MARGERY KEMPE'S STANDING	
a)	Julian of Norwich and Margery Kempe - Contemporaries Compared	95
b)	Margery Kempe - A Milestone	106
VI	A ROOM OF ONE'S OWN	119
VII	SEARCH FOR SUCCESSORS TO MARGERY KEMPE	
a)	The Fate of the *Book*	125
b)	Women Writing (15th to 17th Centuries)	127
VIII	MARY ASTELL	
a)	Mary Astell's Claim for Further Consideration	141
b)	Mary Astell - A Professional Writer	142
c)	Mary Astell's Contribution to Literature and the Status of Women	153
IX	MARGERY KEMPE - THE FIRST ENGLISH FEMINIST	175
X	BIBLIOGRAPHY	
a)	Primary Sources	183
b)	Secondary Sources	186

I INTRODUCTION

English women writers from the Middle Ages to 1700 have received considerably less attention than later authoresses. Traditionally, scholars were content to accept Julian of Norwich as the literary highlight of the earlier part of that period. With some justification, her contemporary, Margery Kempe, though credited with the first autobiography in English, was attributed less merit both as a writer and a mystic.

My initial project was to scrutinize prose written in England by women before 1700 in the light of Virginia Woolf's view that the essential requirement for writing is a "room of one's own".[1] This approach has provided ample evidence to support her claim.

Her assertion can almost certainly be applied to men as well as women. However, one feature common to all the women writers I studied seems to have been some form of suffering. I submit the hypothesis that some form of deprivation is the prerequisite trigger essential for defining a private sphere and thus making creativity possible. My strongest evidence came from the least likely text: *The Book of Margery Kempe*. As a rider to my original theme I became convinced that the frustrations she addressed still confront women today.

---

[1] Virginia Woolf, *A Room of One's Own* (1929; London: Grafton, 1987)

Mary Astell has been dubbed the first English feminist, but my research leads me to claim the title for Margery Kempe, her predecessor by almost three centuries.[1]

In my approach to women writers from the Middle Ages until 1700 I have selected three for special study: Julian of Norwich, Margery Kempe, and Mary Astell.[2]

For chronological reasons, I shall start out with Julian of Norwich, the first known female writer in the English language.

Following a resumé of her personal background and work, I intend to discuss in greater depth specific aspects such as her status as a woman at that time, influences on her development, the reasons for her writing, her place in literature, her style, and, most important, what she had to say. After a short introduction to mediaeval mysticism, I shall consider Margery Kempe in her own right and contrast her *Book* with Julian of Norwich's *Revelations of Divine Love*.

Prolonged perusal of subsequent writers led me to realize that while every authoress substantiates some aspects of Virginia Woolf's claim, only the writings of Mary Astell are relevant to both aspects of my thesis. After a detailed consideration of Mary Astell's work written before 1700, I shall conclude by comparing her standing to the achievements of Margery Kempe.

---

[1] All through this thesis the expression "feminism" and its related terms are used in their widest sense. I imply a "doctrine advocating social and political rights for women equal to those of men" (Random House Dictionary)

[2] I refer to all writers by their full names because I wish to pay respect to these authoresses.

Abbreviations Used in the Text:

LT	*Revelations of Divine Love* or *A Book of Showings to the Anchoress Julian of Norwich*, Long Text
ST	*Revelations of Divine Love* or *A Book of Showings to the Anchoress Julian of Norwich*, Short Text
BMK	*The Book of Margery Kempe*
BMK II	*The Book of Margery Kempe,* Part II
PROP	Mary Astell, *A Serious Proposal to the Ladies*, Part I
PROP II	Mary Astell, *A Serious Proposal to the Ladies*, Part II
LG	Mary Astell, *Letters Concerning the Love of God*
R U M	Mary Astell, *Some Reflections Upon Marriage*

II   JULIAN OF NORWICH

a)   Introduction

Julian of Norwich has inspired many readers and writers both as a figure and with her *Revelations*. Her best known feature is the optimistic assurance to all her Christian brethren that "all will be well", a promise spoken by Christ Himself. She was an anchoress known only by her devotional pseudonym and is thought to have been born in East Anglia, an assumption based merely on "lack of contrary evidence".[1] Little biographical data can be gleaned from the text, and no sources that could give more information have been found so far.

In her *Dictionary of British Women Writers,* Janet Todd calls her the "only British woman generally accepted as a great mystic of the medieval church" (p 373).

Julian of Norwich's famous mystical work, *Revelations of Divine Love*, a record of visions experienced after a miraculous recovery from illness, has earned great praise as a literary contribution and for its religious value.

Two accounts of the anchoress's experiences exist. The First, or Short Version, often referred to as the Short Text, is a recording of the actual visions and was composed soon after Julian of Norwich recovered from the illness for which she had prayed in her youth. After reliving the moments of glory for over two decades (see chap 51/chap 86) she created the Long Version with all the insights that she had acquired through meditation

---

[1] Edmund Colledge and James Walsh, eds., *A Book of Showings to the Anchoress Julian of Norwich.* (Toronto: Pontifical Institute of Mediaeval Studies, 1978) p 7. All quotations will be from this text and refer to chapter and lines. All chapter numbers refer to the Long Text (LT), also known as the Long Version. Any references to the Short Text (ST), or Short Version, will be indicated.

with the help of the Lord. This Second Version analyzes the meanings of her extraordinary interview with the Divine. Parts of the original were omitted; new passages were added. In this Long Text, she explained her experiences more extensively and interwove commentary and description. Where the first text is lively and immediate, the Long Version is more detached and elaborate.

Julian of Norwich's recognition as a mystic is undisputed: "Her assurance and firmness are the strongest testimony to her veracity".[1] Scholarly appraisal refers to her "sense of balance, her humility, her deep c harity, her sane theology displayed so unostentatiously" (Gray,"Mystical Writings" p 334). She is described as "a visionary of remarkable literary and imaginative powers and a compassionate, fascinatingly complex human being."[2] Evelyn Underhill called her "theodidacta, profunda, ecstatica" and "author of the most beautiful of all English mystical works."[3] Though full of praise, Douglas Gray grants her no originality and points out that she was mainly reflecting literary impressions of the day and that "close study reveals that every page is a tissue of scriptural phrases" (Gray, "Mystical Writings" p 334)

Sister Mary Madelva and others have pointed out that T.S. Eliot quoted Julian of Norwich.[4] In chapter 13 of the Short

[1] Douglas Gray, "Mystical Writings: *The Cloud of Unknowing*; Hilton; Julian of Norwich", *The Oxford History of English Literature, vol 1* (1986; Oxford: Clarendon, 1990) pp 324.

[2] Katharina Wilson, "Julian of Norwich", *An Encyclopedia of British Women Writers,* eds. Paul Schlueter and June Schlueter (Chicago and London: St James Press, 1988) p 264.

[3] Evelyn Underhill, *Mysticism* (1911; London: Methuen, 1960) p 467.

[4] Sister Mary Madelva, "Dame Julian of Norwich," *English Studies* 11(1955): pp 21-32.

Version, Julian of Norwich's inquiries after the meaning of sin in God's plan of salvation were answered with: "Synne is behouelye" (52) and, extended through years of meditation, the anchoress presented her conclusion in the Long Version in chapter 27, in the exact words that the poet used in his *Four Quartets*, "Little Gidding", III: "Synne is behouely, but alle shalle be wele, and alle shalle be wele, and alle manner of thynge shalle be wele" (33-34). While experts seem to agree on Julian of Norwich's outstanding theological and literary qualities, in the following sections, I shall attempt an analysis of her work, considering such issues as her motivation for transgressing traditional boundaries by breaking silence, the personality of the writer, her literary achievements, and the possible importance of the *Revelations of Divine Love* for the development of a liberation of women.

b)   The Life and Visions of Julian of Norwich

Julian of Norwich gave the date for her visions as May 13th, 1373. As she asked for her sickness at the age of thirty, this places her date of birth at around 1342 or 1343. We cannot be so specific about the date of her death. She must have been alive in 1393 because the later version of the *Revelations*, was not written "For twenty yere after the tyme of the shewyng saue thre monthys" (chap 51: 86). In a will dating from 1415 a bequest was made to someone called "le ankeres in ecclesia sancti Juliani". This could mean that she was still living even then. However, a possibility exists that the will may refer to another recluse who had taken her place in the annex of the church. More tangible proof for the existence of Julian of Norwich seems to lie in *The Book of Margery Kempe*, whose author went to see "Dame Jelyan" for spiritual guidance:

13

> þe ankres, heryng þe meruelyows goodnes of owyr Lord, hyly thankyd God wyth al hir hert for hys visitacyon, cownselyng þis creatur to be obedyent to þe wyl of owyr Lord & fulfyllyn wyth al hir myghtys what-euyr he put in hir sowle yf it wer not a-geyn þe worshep of God & profyte of hir euyncristen, for, yf it wer, þan it wer nowt þe mevyng of a good spyryte but raþar of an euyl spyrit.[1]

In the course of the sixth centenary celebrations Julian of Norwich was included in the Church of England calendar. Ironically, scribal error changed XIII to VIII - May eighth, instead of thirteenth (the actual date of her visions), is now St Julian's day.[2]

The author of the *Revelations of Divine Love* called herself "unlettyrde" (chap 2: 1). Douglas Gray interprets the epithet as a "captatio benevolentiae" ("Mystical Writings" p 322). Possibly her use of "illiterate" meant being able to read but not write in Latin. On the other hand experts like Sister Anna Maria Reynolds and Wolfgang Riehle consider her writing in the vernacular evidence that she knew no Latin.[3] In this case, calling herself unlettered could be seen as an anticipation of possible accusations against a woman for writing down and making

---

[1] Margery Kempe, *The Book of Margery Kempe*, eds. Sanford Brown Meech, and Hope Emily Allen (1940; Oxford: Oxford University Press 1982) chap 18.

[2] Clifton Wolters, trans. and intro., *Julian of Norwich. Revelations of Divine Love* (Harmondsworth: Penguin,1966) In this Modern English rendering of the *Revelations*, Clifton Wolters gives the date of the visions as May eighth, in contradiction to the actual text, but according to the CoE calendar.

[3] Sister Anna Maria Reynolds, "Some Literary Influences on the Revelations of Julian of Norwich,". *Leeds Se* 7/8(1952): pp 18-28.

Wolfgang Riehle, *The Middle English Mystics,* trans. Bernhard Standring (1977; London: Routledge and Kegan Paul, 1981)

public her experiences. Her intimate knowledge of contemporary texts such as the anonymous *Cloud of Unknowing*, Hilton's *Scale of Perfection*, and Richard Rolle's *Fire of Love* seems to indicate that she read English with ease. As a student at a convent, as a novice or nun and as an anchoress she would have had access to monastic libraries.

Norwich at that time was a market town famous for its wool trade with Flanders. With the wool trade, the Beguines, whose speciality was the dying of wool, came to England. Theirs is a Flemish order according to whose rules property is retained and vows can be revoked any time. Julian of Norwich could have got her religious training from them.

Alternatively, it is possible that she was educated in the Benedictine convent at Carrow outside Norwich. Benedictines are not basically proselytizing so the young woman may have gone to their convent school without necessarily becoming a novice.

Julian of Norwich repeatedly referred to the "A B C" (e.g. chap 80: 11), so she almost certainly had some scholastic training. Only through intense private studies could she have acquired that level of familiarity that allows for Evelyn Underhill's appreciation: "In her the best gifts of Rolle and Hilton are transmuted by a 'genius for the infinite' " (p 467).

The anchoress may have been of merchant, even aristocratic stock. The sickness she had prayed for as a girl specified that it should occur "in my jowth, that I might haue it when I ware xxxth yeare olde" (chap 2: 38-39). Since peasants of thirty were not considered young, her phrasing could indicate that she came from a higher level of society, for better conditions of life and less work would allow for greater life expectancy. Her description of the seating at the Lord's table in chapter 51

15

suggests some knowledge of courtly manners and lends further substance to this conjecture.

Maybe her own family was in the cloth trade - the usage of the technical term "flammyng", which stands for a particular kind of stitch, would suggest it.[1] Furthermore, her description of the Lord's coat shows an awareness of colour and of the texture of fabric:

> The blewhed of the clothyng betokenyth his stedfastnesse, the brownhed of his feyer face with the semely blackhede of the eyen was most according to shew his holy sobyrnesse, the largnesse of his clothyng, whych was feyer flammyng about, betokenyth *p*at he hath beclosyd in hym all hevyns and all endlesse joy and blysse; and this was shewed in a touch, wher I saw that my vnderstandyng was led into the lorde. (chap 51: 153-159)

Given the relations between Norwich and Flanders, Julian of Norwich could have been aware of fashion trends either through her family or her connections to a Beguine convent. Possibly, however, her vocabulary simply echoed the idiom of a mediaeval cloth trading center.

When a young girl, the author of the *Revelations of Divine Love* felt a great desire to suffer in the same manner as St Cecilia, the Roman martyr, whose story was known in England from Chaucer's "Second Nun's Tale". Making three wishes, she asked God for "mynd of the passion" (i.e true understanding of His passion in order to share the sufferings of the Marys at Calvary), "bodilie sicknes" as an ouward sign (i.e. to receive the sacrament of extreme unction, to be as close to death, as close to

---

[1] See Joan Fisher, *The Creative Art of Needlepoint"* (London: Hamlyn, 1972)

God as possible), and "to have of godes gyfte thre woundys" as the expression of inward suffering (i.e. the wounds of true contrition, genuine compassion, and sincere longing for God) (chap 2: 5-6).

Through her most intense wish, to be ill to the point of death, she hoped to be wholly cleansed through the mercy of God:

> I would that that sicknes were so hard as to the death, that I might in that sicknes haue vndertaken all my rightes of the holie church, my selfe weeniyng that I should haue died, and that all creatures might suppose þe same that saw me; for I would haue no maner of comforte of fleshly ne erthely life in that sicknes. I desyred to haue al maner of paynes, bodily and ghostly, that I should haue if I should haue died, all the dredys and temptations of fiendes, and alle maner of other paynes, saue the out passing of the sowle. And this ment I for I would be purgied by the mercie of god, and after liue more to the worshippe of god by cause of that sicknes.
> (chap 2: 21-31)

The desire for purging could be the result of a personal experience or a reflection of the concept of the wretchedness of the human body. I base my interpretation of her wish to suffer on the assumption that at some time in her early youth Julian of Norwich, like Margery Kempe, committed what she or society may have considered a grave sin. Judging from the text it seems likely that her education took place in a highly religious environment, with sin and forgiveness an omnipresent theme. Relief, according to the dogma of the Church, was possible. By suffering and withdrawing she could approach redemption in an

17

accepted way. Furthermore, this intense wish can be seen as proof for her extraordinary character which was finally exceptional enough to make her into an authoress.

In spite of these morbid wishes, there is no indication of an unbalanced mind. Where a hypochondriac would have dwelt on a detailed description of the sickness, the future anchoress referred only briefly to her physical condition in the moments before the miraculous healing. Even in her highest transport, her expression remained controlled. Hence, as Douglas Gray points out, no "bizarre legends" (e.g. of eccentricity) are linked to her name ("Mystical Writings" p 334).

The first fulfillment of her wishes occurred when she was thirty and a half years old. She became very ill, was expected to die and recovered by concentrating on the crucifix. During the night and day following her return to health, she experienced the "endles blisse made in XVI shewynges" (chap 1: 2-3) of God's unconditional love for humankind. These *Revelations of Divine Love* she wrote down soon after in what was to become known as the Short Version. Already in this first description she expressed her most famous lesson "that alle manere of thynge schalle be wele" (ST chap XV: 30). This conviction was to become the central theme in her message to her fellow Christians.

Possibly in order to contemplate the visions and to live a life of devotion, she became an anchoress and withdrew into the cell at St Julian's church in Norwich. She may have taken the name from the church where she lived, as was the custom of the times.

Through a long series of evaluations of the basic showings and meditations on the meaning of the visions, Julian of Norwich gained the certainty of God's ultimate forgiveness through love which she expressed in the final passage of the Long Version.

The way of life of an anchoress is described in detail in *The Ancrene Riwle* , generally attributed to St Aeldred, the abbot of Rievaulx (1146-1166), who wrote the book for his own sisters. The conditions of life for a recluse were relatively comfortable. Initiation rites resembled closely those of a burial. The woman actually was anointed. After the ceremony she was led into the cell where she would spend the rest of her days. Julian of Norwich did say: "This place is pryson, this lyfe is pennance" (chap 77: 41) but whether she actually referred to her dwelling is unclear. To both the outer world and the church itself the anchoress was connected by a window so she could follow mass and talk to people who came to her for spiritual guidance. She was allowed servants. She had a little garden, sometimes even a cow.

It is difficult to say what made Julian of Norwich choose the life of a recluse. Was it her own will? She did receive extreme unction in the course of her illness. Could she have felt this sacrament to have deeper significance? Did she interpret the ritual as the outward physical sign of inner spiritual grace? Once she realized she was not going to die she may have wanted her life to be as close to death, as close to God as possible.

Was her choice an available alternative to an arranged marriage? Could it perhaps indicate disappointment with some experiences in her life? Julian of Norwich seems to have taken every possible precaution not to reveal her identity. Only occasional passages allow glances at a possibly unhappy life before her retreat. The fierce physicality in the description of the fiend in chapter 67 could reflect an actual incident in Julian of Norwich's life:

> Ande in my slepe at the begynnyng me thought the fende sett hym in my throte, putting forth a vysage

fulle nere my face lyke a yonge man, and it was longe and wonder leen. I saw nevyr none such; the coloure was reed, lyke þe tylle stone whan it is new brent, with blacke spottes there in lyke frakylles, fouler than þe tyle stone. His here was rede as rust, not scoryd fore, with syde lockes hangyng on þe thonwonges. He grynnyd vpon me with a shrewde loke, shewed me whyt teth and so mekylle me thought it the more vgly. Body ne handes had he none shaply, but with hys pawes he helde me in the throte, and woulde a stoppyd my breth and kylde me, but he myght not. (1-11)

An initial reading of the Long Text of the *Divine Revelations of Love to the Anchoress Julian of Norwich* indicates no awareness of sexuality. In her own light she appears colourless, lifeless, devoid of gender. However, Robert H. Thouless, as early as 1924, dealt with the fact that diabolical visions often indicate the reemergence of a suppressed sexuality.[1] In the case of Julian of Norwich, the body, weakened by sickness, would have allowed this relaxing of control. Furthermore, "this ugly shewyng was made sleepyng, and so was none other" (chap 67:12). Hidden fears might have caused what would, in this case, have to be termed a nightmare. Such a psychological interpretation points to hitherto unsuspected events in the past of Julian of Norwich and lends substance to my suspicions concerning the causes underlying her wish for suffering.

But she also used the austerity of an earthly mother to contrast and accentuate the loving warmth of Jesus as mother:

---

[1] Robert H. Thouless, *The Lady Julian.* A Psychological Study (London: SPCK, 1924)

> And though oure erthly moder may suffer her chylde to peryssch, oure hevynly moder Jhesu may nevyr suffer us þat be his chyldren to peryssch. (chap 61: 37-39)

If we are ready to consider unfulfilled love a viable cause, parental neglect could have been the reason for her withdrawing. The latter suggestion, if substantiated, would give added insight into Julian of Norwich's perception of God as the ideal mother figure, an aspect that will be dealt with in a later section.

Whatever the reasons for her chosen lifestyle, she was in complete accordance with her age. As a deeply religious person she spent a large part of her youth in church surrounded by an atmosphere of devotion and visual richness. Now, as then, young people are susceptible to the mysteries of religion. The impact that reading or hearing about continental women mystics such as St Cecilia, St Bridget of Sweden, and St Catherine of Siena made on her can be seen in the close resemblance of Julian of Norwich's experiences to the pattern of their mystical lives. However, despite the many similarities, the anchoress managed to show an impressive independence. Furthermore, she has earned her place in literature. Not only did she experience her visions, she also wrote about them and through her prose made her "Union with the Absolute" (Underhill p 23) accessible.

According to Evelyn Underhill's theory, she is a true mystic because true mysticism is always cradled in dogma. Reading Julian of Norwich's text, we find frequent protestations of orthodoxy. Possibly the numerous allusions to her loyalty were included to ensure her safety. An intelligent woman, she was aware of witchhunts and took every possible precaution not to become a victim. Yet her belief in what she had seen was strong enough to persuade her to encroach on male territory and, through the *Revelations*, share what she had learnt with her beloved fellow Christians. As this writing seems to be the sole digression of a woman who in every other way lived up to male criteria, there was no reason why she should be attacked.

The authenticity of her visions is undoubted. Desires such as a wish for lethal sickness seem unwholesome and extreme today, yet there is no sign of hysteria in Julian of Norwich.[1] Maybe her perception of the demands of a society where women submitted to the point of self denial included desires such as a wish for mortal illness.

In her cell, she processed her divine experience and the development from the Short Text to the Long Text can be compared to a change from vision to actual revelation, from the descriptive to the didactic. Through the reworking of what she had seen she was able to communicate implicitly guidepoints to basic problems of a Christian life. "She closes and crowns English mediaeval mysticism. She was a seer, a lover, and a poet" (Underhill 467).

c) The Text of Julian of Norwich's
Revelations of Divine Love

A Book of Showings to the Anchoress Julian of Norwich or *Revelations of Divine Love* is the first work written by a woman under her own name in England. If she had a scribe, it seems likely that he adhered closely to what was dictated to him. By calling herself "unlettered", and by omitting all reference to herself as a woman from the Long Version, Julian of Norwich demonstrated extreme modesty. The same trait of character and

---

[1] All through this thesis the expression "hysteria" is used in its widest sense. I imply a highly emotional and irrational state.

her careful anticipation of accusations would most probably have made her mention any help given.

She was informed that the divine inspirations were meant "generally" and illustrated her insight with an episode from her own travails:

> And whan god almyghty had shewyd so plentuosly and so fully of hys goodnesse, I desyred to wytt of a serteyn creature *p*at I louyd yf it shulde contynue in good levyng, whych I hopyd by the grace of god was begonne; and in this syngular desyer it semyd that I lettyd my selfe, for I was nott taught in thys tyme. And then I was answeryd in my reson, as it were by a frendfulle mene: Take it generally and beholde the curtesy of thy lorde god as he shewyd to the, for it is more worshype to god to beholde hym in alle than in any specyalle thyng. I assentyd, and ther with I lernyd *p*at it is more wurshyppe to god to know althyng in generalle than to lyke in ony thyng in specialle. And if I shuld do wysely after thys techang I shuld nott by glad for any thyng in specialle, ne gretly dyssesyd for any manner thyng, for alle shalle be wele; for the fulhed of joy is to beholde god in alle. (chap 35: 2-14)

Her intuition led her to conclude that the *Revelations* were made "generally" in every respect. Clearly, they were meant for circulation:

> For truly I saw and vnderstode in oure lordes menyng that he shewde it for he wyll haue it knowyn more than it is. (chap 86: 7-9)

23

They were not published until after her death. In the last chapter we read: "This boke is begonne by goddys gyfte and his grace, but it is nott yett performyd, as to my syght" (1-2). Declining strength may have caused the anchoress to write this sentence and since no further chapter has been added, we may assume that Julian of Norwich, who must have been over sixty by then, died before she was able to finish her work.

The only known copy of the Short Version is included in a collection of mediaeval devotional texts in the British Library (MSS Add. 37790). It was written in many different hands around the middle of the fifteenth century and is probably the product of a monastic scriptorium.

Three manuscript copies of the Long Version survive. Two seem to have been written around the end of the seventeenth century and are preserved in the British Library (MSS Sloane 2499 and 3705). The third copy, to be found in the Bibliothèque Nationale in Paris (No 40 Fonds Anglais), has been dated by Clifton Wolters at around 1500 (p 13). However, Edmund Colledge and James Walsh claim that the manuscript is written in "a sedulous, but unskilled and unconvincing imitation ... of a hand of c. 1500" (p 7). In their opinion it was copied in the seventeenth century.

The earliest printed edition was published by Serenus Cressy in 1670, apparently for the use of the English Benedictine nuns in France, under the title: *Sixteen Revelations of Divine Love, Shewed To a Devout Servant of Our Lord called Mother Juliana, an Anchorete of Norwich: who lived in the Dayes of King Edward the Third*

It is generally assumed, and I follow this assumption, that the Long Version is an amplification of the Short Version as it contains conclusions to which Julian of Norwich must have come during her twenty years in the anchorage. Clifton Wolters, however, suggests that the Short Version could just as well be a distillation of the Long Version.

d)   Julian of Norwich's Processing of the Visions

The *Revelations* have earned praise for their style as well as for their contents.[1] However, style and content of Julian of Norwich's showings cannot be analyzed separately. Although the second version is an extension of the first record of the visions produced in twenty years of intense preoccupation with their meaning, I do not intend to compare the Long Version with the Short Version unless there is some additional insight to be reached through the collation of the two texts.

In order to understand what Julian of Norwich was trying to tell her fellow Christians we have to try to understand the mechanism of her seeing. After all, there is the possibility that her experiences could have been the result of her prolonged illness, and perhaps delirium due to lack of food. The visions could have been induced by the ecstasy of the last rites. Or were her perceptions a kind of self hypnotizing provoked by the passionate desire to perceive the Almighty in all His glory?

Chapter 1 of the *Revelations of Divine Love* sketches the contents of the respective showings. The first vision was fundamental, and the interpretations of all the following ones were based on it.

---

[1]   For a further study on Julian of Norwich's style see:
Sister Mary Arthur Knowlton, *The Influence of Richard Rolle and of Julian of Norwich on the Middle English Lyrics* (The Hague: Mouton, 1973)

Robert K. Stone, *Middle English Prose Style: Margery Kempe and Julian of Norwich* (The Hague: Mouton, 1970)

For a detailed analysis of Julian of Norwich's rhetorical figures, I refer the reader to the appendix of the Colledge/Walsh edition, pp 735-748.

Julian of Norwich experienced the first fifteen showings in a waking state and without interruption:

> Now haue I tolde you of xv shewynges, as god whytsafe to minyster them to my mynde, renewde by lyghtenynges and touchynges, I hope of the same spiryte that shewyth them alle. Of whych xv shewynges þe furst beganne erly in þe mornynge, about the oure of iiij, and it lastyd shewyng by processe, full feyer and soberly, eche folowyng other, tylle it was none of þe day or paste. (chap 65: 35-40)

The sixteenth Revelation was given during the ensuing night; unlike the first fifteen, it was made to her in her sleep. She saw it as a confirmation of the previous ones:

> Ande after this the goode lorde shewde the xvj revelation on the nyght folowyng, as I shalle sey after; whych xvj was conclusyon and confirmation to all the xv. (chap 66: 3-5)

The visions were induced by Julian of Norwich's concentrating on the face of Christ. The focus of her experience remained the dying Christ, His Passion. Her interpretations, however, were influenced by her primary and most important lesson that "all will be well".

She divided her insights - perhaps following the trend of numerical classification - into three different kinds:

> Alle this blessyd techyng of oure lorde god was shewde by thre partys, that is to sey by bodely syght, and by worde formyd in myne understandynge, and by gostely syghte. For þe bodely syghte, I haue

> seyde as I sawe, as truly as I can. And for þe words, I haue seyde them ryghte as oure lorde shewde them me. And for the gostely syghte, I haue seyde some dele, but I may nevyr fulle telle it; and therfore of this gostely syght I am steryd to sey more, as god wylle geue me grace. (chap 73: 1-8)

The way she received her divine inspirations of the third kind is explained more fully in chapter 9:

> But the goostely syght I can nott ne may shew it as openly ne as fully as I would. But trust in our lord god almightie that he shall of his godnes and for iour loue make yow to take it more ghostely and more sweetly then I can or may tell it.
> (29-34)

If we assume the "bodyly syght" to be the first stage of her elucidation, then the "words formyd in myne vnderstondyng" are the articulation of what she actually saw, the result of the process of digesting her impressions, the assimilation of the visions by the power of her intellect. The "goostely syght", however, must be, by definition, a deeper understanding, a personal thing, impossible to communicate in all its dimension.

As Sister Christina von Nolcken points out, these three modes of revelation correspond in a general sense with what had become a tradition in the style of St Augustine.[1] No doubt they would meet Julian of Norwich's urge to catalogue her experiences according to some system. Moreover, I consider the fact that she had three different kinds of perception a possible reflection of the everpresent trinity.

---

[1] Sister Christina von Nolcken, "Julian of Norwich," 1984. *Middle English Prose. A Critical Guide to Major Authors and Genres.* ed. A.S.G. Edwards (New Brunswick NJ: Rutgers University Press, 1986) p 103.

Although Evelyn Underhill points out that mysticism is something normal, today it may seem problematic to see a mystic as completely sane. Compounding the problem is Julian of Norwich's rather striking wish for suffering. Yet on the other hand, she rationally edited her visions. She introduced cross-references such as "as it is before seyde" (chaps 8: 14-15 and 40: 25), and "I haue seyde at the begynnyng, wher it seyth..." (chap 66: 6-7).

In addition, the controlled expression of rapture in the *Revelations of Divine Love* makes it difficult to dismiss the author. Although she was extraordinary, no critic, mediaeval or modern, has called her mad or even drawn attention to any eccentricity in the way it was done with her contemporary, Margery Kempe.

Her text is in the mystical tradition of the middle ages:

> Each mystic, original though he be, yet owes much to the inherited acquirement of his spiritual ancestors. These ancestors form his tradition, are the classic examples on which his education is based; and from them he takes the language which they have sought out and constructed as a means of telling their adventures to the world.
> (Underhill p 454)

She dealt with a problem common to all mystics: she was trying to communicate something basically incommunicable:

> The nomber of the words passyth my wyttes and my understandyng and alle my myghtes, for they were in *þ*e hyghest, as to my syght, for ther in is comprehendyd I can not telle what; but the joy that I saw in the shewyng of them passyth alle that hart can thynk or soule may desire. (chap 26: 11-15)

Possibly her pronounced use of enumeration was another result of a deep need to express the ineffable - to find earthly order in unearthly experience.

The presentation of the *Revelations* reflects the lifestyle of the author. Calm in character and graced with a determined mind, leading an outwardly undisturbed life while striving to reach her goal, she was able to formulate clear thoughts and come to logical conclusions. As a result, her work corresponds to the patterns of continental mystical literature, yet shows impressive independence.

The anchoress at Norwich was eclectic: she was prepared to ignore or accept advice according to her own beliefs. The anonymous author of *The Cloud of Unknowing*, who may have influenced the author of the *Revelations*, wrote:

> For if those who mean to become contemplatives, spiritual and inward looking, reckon they ought to hear, smell, see, taste, or feel spiritual things in external visions or in the depth of their being, they

> are seriously misled, and are working against the natural order of things. For the natural order is that by the senses we should gain our knowledge of the outward, material world, but not thereby acquire our knowledge of things spiritual.[1]

Julian of Norwich's writing shows two significant points of discrepancy. She believed that reason belonged inseparably to man:

> Theyse iij propertees were seen in oone goodnesse, in to whych goodnesse my reson wolde be oonyd and clevyng to with alle ƥe myghtes. I beheldc with reverent drede, and hyghly mervelyng in the syght and in feelyng of the swete accorde that our reson is in god, vnderstandyng that it is ƥe hyghest gyfte that we haue receyuyd, and it is growndyd in kynd.
> (chap 83: 8-13)

The insistence that mind and spirit are not in opposition, indeed that they interpenetrate, shows a fundamental readiness to diverge from established mystical doctrine.

Her introduction of sensuous imagery can be seen as further repudiation of her predecessor's advice. For example, in her *Revelations* she, without compunction, appealed through metaphor to the senses of smell, feeling, and hearing. The Lord she experienced as "delectably smellyng" (chap 43: 53). The devil's apparition was accompanied by "greete heet and a foule stynch" (chap 67: 17). Furthermore, in chapter 14 she described heaven as the house of the Lord in terms that would clearly not have been acceptable to the author of the *Cloud of Unknowing*:

---

[1] Betty Radice, trans. and ed., *The Cloud of Unknowing* (1967; London: Penguin Books, 1985) p 145.

> I saw hym ryally reigne in hys howse, and all fulfyllyth it with joy and myrth, hym selfe endlesly to glad and solace hys derewurthy frendes fulle homely and fulle curtesly, with mervelous melody in endlesse loue in hys awne feyer blessydfulle chere, which glorious chere of the godhede fulfyllyth alle hevyn of ioy and blysse. (7-12)

Whatever sources influenced Julian of Norwich, "by the time she wrote, she had so assimilated them that they were part and parcel of her thinking" (Wolters p 19). The most important aspect in the following consideration of style, however, is, that her application of stylistic elements never took precedence over her main goal which was the interpretation of the visions.

Frequently, Julian of Norwich stressed passages by using alliteration: "...he shulde haue no myschevous felyng ne no maner steryng, no sorowyng that servyth to synne" (chap 47: 20-21). However, the use of repeating and playing upon the same letter does not necessarily point to any particular influence, for it was common usage in Anglo-Saxon verse, such as "Judith" (55 ff), "The Dream of the Rood" (10 ff) and any number of mediaeval texts, e.g. "The Lay of Havelok the Dane" from the thirteenth century. From earliest youth she must have been assimilating the homiletic techniques of the preacher. In her sentence structure she habitually followed a forthright opening in the affirmative or interrogative with either illustration or paraphrase.

On occasion her diction is elevated to match the ecstasy of the visions. Rhythmic passages add to the feeling of elation.

> And marcy is a werkyng þat comyth of the goodnes of god, and it shalle last wurkynge as long as synne is suffered to pursew ryghtfulle soules. And whan synne hath no lenger leue to pursew, than shalle the werkyng of mercy cees. And than shalle alle be brought into ryghtfulnes and ther in stonde withouȝte ende. By his sufferannce we falle, and in hys blessyd loue with his myght and hys wysdom we are kept, and by mercy and grace we be reysyd to manyfolde more joy. (chap 35: 37-43)

Long lists of attributes result in a pattern characteristic of the chanting practised in eastern religions and in Psalms. This stylistic figure was used by other mystics such as Richard Rolle.[1] Her readiness for repetition can be illustrated by the following passage:

> This dede and thys werke abowt oure saluation was ordeyned as wele as god myght ordeyne it. It was don as wurshypfully as Crist myght do it; and heer I saw a full blysse in Crist, for his blysse shuld nott haue ben fulle yf it myght ony better haue ben done than it was done. (chap 22: 53-57)

An awareness of stress in her didactic manner is obvious in the next quotation:

> I saw in Crist that the father is. The werkyng of the father is this: that he giveth mede to hys sonne Jhesu Crist. This gyft and this mede is so blyssydfulle to Jhesu that his father myght haue geavyn hym no mede that myght haue lykeyd to hym better." (chap 23: 13-17)

---

[1] "The Form of Living": "Contemplatyfe lyfe es mykel inwarde, and forþi it es lastandar and sykerar, restfuller, delitabiler, luflyer, and mare medeful."

This playing on the same word is due to no paucity of vocabulary, but is a clear element of style. She proved herself to be perfectly able to reiterate an idea through the use of synonym: "It is a joy, a blysse, an endlesse lykyng...." (chap 22: 5-6). Incorporating her readiness to stress an idea through repetition with persuasive lyrical tone, she regularly chose pairs or strings of adjectives: "Thys syght was fulle swete and mervelous to beholde, pesyble and restfull, suer and delectabyll" (chap 55: 43-45).

Frequently she gave an uplifting tone to her culminating phrases

> Alle þe soules that shalle be savyd in hevyn withou3t ende be ryghtfulle in the sy3t of god and by hys awne goodnesse, in whych ryghtfullnes we be endlessly kepte and marvelously aboue all creatures. (chap 35: 33-36)

Auditory devices such as the assonantal "reuerend drede" (chap 7: 7) are proof for her 'ear for language' and her treating readers as members of a congregation.

The language she used to describe her experience is abstract rather than representational. The few exceptions, such as the depiction of the Lord's coat and the detailed observation of the servants clothing in chapter 51, as well as the representations of Christ dying on the cross, produce the same powerful effect as do the ecstatic passages in otherwise calm sections. A passage in chapter 28 exemplifies this impressive technique: "Holy chyrch shalle be shakyd in sorow and anguyssch and trybulacion in this worlde as man shakyth a cloth in the wynde" (1-3). Close investigation into her descriptions reveals that Julian of Norwich did indeed process manifold impressions in her mystic state.

33

Taking further a point already made, recollections of daily life in Norwich influenced not only her choice of vocabulary but also the vehicle of her metaphor. Describing the bleeding head of Christ in His passion, she likened the drops of blood to

> the droppes of water that falle of the evesyng of an howse after a grete shower of reyne, that falle so thycke that no man may nomber them with no bodely wyt. And for the roundnesse they were lyke to the scale of heryng in the spredyng of the forhede. (chap 7: 22-24)

The anchoress had the gift of uniting abstract thoughts with everyday words. Her sudden interjections of the minutiae of daily life into passages of theological importance jolt the reader with their immediacy. When cruelly tormented by the devil she specified that he stayed with her "alle nyght and on the morrow tylle it was about pryme day" (chap 70: 11-12). Even more mundane is her description of the perfect creation of man and his bodily functions:

> A man goyth vppe ryght and the soule of his body is sparyde as a purse fulle feyer. And whan it is tyme of his nescessery, it is openyde and sparyde ayen fulle honestly. And that it is that doyth this, it is schewed ther wher he seyth he comyth downe to vs to the lowest parte of oure nede. For he hath no dispite of that he made, ne he hath no dysdeyne to serue vs at the symplyst office that oure body longyth in kynde, for loue of the soule that he made to his awne lycknesse. (chap 6: 35-41)

Passages like this lead us to a side issue which will take on greater importance when we examine studies of Margery

Kempe's *Book*. What I term "condescending criticism" probably influenced Clifton Wolters' editing. He states in his introduction to the Modern English version of Julian of Norwich's *Revelations of Divine Love* that

> translators take the occasional liberty when seeking to put an author into contemporary language, but to do so here [...] would seem to the present Editor to confuse freedom with license. And so he has sought to translate 'warts and all'. (p 20)

Nevertheless he simply left out the part dealing with defecation. Such reservations seem wholly unreasonable. Prudishness about representations of this sort did not exist then. In an early rendition of Little Red Riding Hood, the little girl quite cleverly uses her need in order to escape from the wolf. She tells the werewolf that she badly has to go outside. To keep her from running away the wolf attaches a rope to her foot. Outside, Little Red Riding Hood ties the rope to a tree and runs away. The werewolf becomes impatient and says: "Are you making a load out there? Are you making a load?"[1] Obviously in the days of Julian of Norwich no negative connotation was connected to bowel movements or similar functions.

The question of a so-called feminine vocabulary must be raised. Let us assume that such a thing does exist. What does it mean? Isn't the choice of words a matter of personality rather than sex? Furthermore, writing was a male preserve. Surely someone as wary as Julian of Norwich would favour a neutral, conventional vocabulary. Her omission of the reference to herself as "a womann leued, febille and fraille" (ST chap 6: 41-42) from

---

[1] Jack Zipes, "A Second Glance at Little Red Riding Hood's Trials and Tribulations". *Don't Bet on the Prince. Contemporary Feminist Fairy Tales in North America and England*, ed. Jack Zipes (Aldershot: Gower,1986) p 126.

the Long Version could indicate a discretion on the subject of her femininity. Therefore, apparent evidence of female authorship must in her case be accidental.

To conclude this consideration of some elements of Julian of Norwich's style, I have chosen a quotation which demonstrates many of the points made above.

> And in thys tyme I sawe a body lyeng on *þe* erth, whych body shewde heuy and feerfulle and with oute shape and forme. as it were a swylge stynkyng myrrhe; and sodeynly oute of this body sprong a fulle feyer creature, a lyttylle chylld, full shapyn and formyd, swyft and lyfly and whytter then the lylye, whych sharpely glydyd vppe in to hevyn.
> The swylge of the body betokenyth grette wretchydnesse of oure dedely flessch; and the lyttylnes of the chylde betokenyth the clennes and the puernesse of oure soule. (chap 64: 31-37)

She used five lines (from the Colledge/Walsh text) to make the statement and two and a half lines to sum up and explain that statement. At the same time she used the resumé to support her argument. Her use of various figures of speech illustrates the discrepancy between physical and spiritual. The deliberate repetition of the word "body" results in a stress on the palpable which is heightened even more when juxtaposed to the last word of the paragraph, "hevyn". This is a typical example of her use of antithesis. The emphatic effect of alliteration in "fulle feyer" and "swylge stynkyng", together with the assonance in "shewde heuy and feerfulle" introduce deliberate sonority and add to the dramatic display of her involvement.

Metaphors such as likening the body to a bog and the soul to the lily augment the inner tension of her reasoning.

Accumulation of adjectives often expressed in pairs e.g. "full shapyn and formyd, swyft and lyfly and whytter then the lylye" illustrate her sense of rhythm and her awareness of the value of sound.

The image of the rotting body is undoubtedly a digest of her own experience. All of Europe had been afflicted by wars and plague. Bodies left unburied for days must have been a common sight, and gruesome reports from the Hundred Years' War, fought on French soil, must have reached England. With the contrasting representation of the child, whiter than the lily, Julian of Norwich appears to have verbalized her firm belief that out of the worst something beautiful and pure can arise. This image follows a traditional iconographic idea: the contemporary painting "La Primavera" by Botticelli, represents a similar situation - Adam lying on the ground after the fall, a white lily growing out of his mouth.

God's prophecy that "all will be well" enabled Julian of Norwich to recognize that the fall of man, in itself the most terrible thing that could happen to mankind, was turned, through God's love for humanity, to the most wonderful gift - the birth of the Saviour. Her vision of the Christ child probably embodied the idea that a woman sees hope in a baby; in German "in der Hoffnung" means pregnant. In modern dream analysis the figure of the child signifies inherent potential. Julian may therefore have been subconsciously aware of her own potential as a woman.

e)   Julian of Norwich's Teachings

Julian of Norwich's fame rests on her ability to extract general truths from her private visions. Not content to relive in solitude the ecstatic joy which she had experienced, she felt driven to make known a general application. As His servant, she wanted to share the particular grace of love with her brethren.

I propose to study five relevant teachings and their distillation in her lasting message.

(i)   Alle schalle be wele

Julian of Norwich's best known doctrine is the optimistic assurance to all her Christian brethren that all will be well, a promise repeatedly spoken by Christ Himself and most convincingly delivered in chapter 31:

> And thus oure good lord answeryd to alle the questyons and dow3tys that I myght make, sayeng full comfortabely; I may make alle thyng wele, and I can make alle thyng welle, and I shalle make alle thyng wele, and I wylle make alle thyng welle; and thou shalt se thy selfe *p*at alle maner of thyng shall be welle. (1-6)

Although she has set down the message in reported speech, attributing it to "oure good lord", Julian of Norwich is persuasively passing on her own positive belief. Using the psalmist's technique of repetition, she invited complacent passivity. In her own case, her message led to an enviable faith and a deep commitment to her mission.

(ii) I it am

An even more exaggerated use of repetition is to be found in the sections where Julian of Norwich reached her deepest understanding of God and His ways. Elevated diction such as the repetition of the phrase "I it am" results in a highly dramatic presentation of her feelings:

> I it am; that is to sey: I it am, the myght and the goodnes of fatherhode, I it am, the wysdom and the kyndnes of the moderhode, I it am, the lyght and the grace that is all blessed loue; I it am, the trynyte, I it am, the unyte; I it am, the hye souereyn goodnesse of all manner thyng, I it am þat makyth the to loue, I it am, that mykyth þe to long, I it am, the endlesse fulfyllyng of all true deseyers. (chap 59: 13-19)[1]

Again, the chanting of the phrase "I it am", together with a choice of words that in themselves create a sense of elation, such as "trinity", "unity" and "sovereign goodness", conjures up an atmosphere of meditation. In these passages of pure exhortation, Julian of Norwich relied on positive statements, eradicating any antithetical tension. Such appealing terms as "the goodness of fatherhood", "the wisdom and kindness of motherhood", "blessed love", "light" and "grace" allow easy identification. Furthermore, the text plays on the basic needs of humankind to be embraced in love.

---

[1] A similar passage is found in chapter 26: "Oftyn tymes oure lorde Jhesu seyde:I it am, I it am. I it am that is hyghest. I it am that thou lovyst. I it am that thou lykyst. I it am that thou servyst. I it am that thou longest. I it am that thou desyryst. I it am that thou menyste. I it am that is alle. I it am that holy church prechyth the and techeyth thee. I it am that shewde me before to the." (6-14)

(iii)   The Scale of God's Love: the Hazelnut

Julian of Norwich did not place any of her visions in an ecclesiastical setting. However, she could not help but digest the impact that church service was bound to have made on her. In the semi-trance of intense prayer, music, incense, and refracted light streaming through church windows must have left extensive imprints on her deeply religious mind. The scale of Norwich's Norman cathedral reminds the mystically inclined worshipper of his own insignificance measured against God's boundless glory. Proportionately, a hazelnut lying in her hand would be visibly dwarfed. This concretion of her concept of God's perfection appears in the oft-quoted passage about the hazelnut where Julian of Norwich displayed her power as a mystic and writer by expressing the inexpressible:

> And in this he shewed a little thing, the quantitie of an haselnott, lying in *þe* palme of my hand, as me semide, and it was as rounde as a balle. I looked theran with the eye of my vnderstandyng and thought: What may this be? And it was answeryd generaelly [sic] thus: It is all that is made. I marvayled how it might laste, for me thought it might sodenly haue fallen to nawght for littlenes. And I was answered in my vnderstanding; It lasteth and ever shall, for god loueth it; and so hath all thing being by the loue of god. (chap 5: 1-16)

Evelyn Underhill described this experience in the following words: "We must pull down our own card houses - descend, as the mystics say, 'into our nothingness' - and examine for ourselves the foundations of all possible human experience...." (p 4). The original visions were induced by Julian of Norwich's concentration on the crucifix. Her contemplating a "little thing, the quantitie of an haselnott" in the emotionally rapt environment would allow for the genuine mystic transport which accentuated the 'Scale of Perfection' of God's caring for humankind.

(iv) Motherhood in God, the Father; God, the Son; and God, the Holy Ghost

A continuous feature in Julian of Norwich's teachings is her interpretation of God as Mother: "As verely as god is oure fader, as verely is god oure moder" (chap 59: 12). As I pointed out earlier, we have to keep in mind the possibility that an unfulfilled desire for animal warmth lies at the bottom of Julian of Norwich's understanding of the motherhood of God in His Unity or in any one of His aspects. "And this was shewed in the first syght and in all, for wher Jhesu appireth the blessed trinitie is vnderstand, as to my sight" (chap 4: 14-16). When writing of the trinity in chapter 54, she played on the basic need of every human being to belong, to be cared for, to be looked after, and to be loved. She used the prototype of the happy family to ensure easy identification, thus creating a sense of security that we would all happily accept.

> For the almyghty truth of the trynyte is oure fader, for he made vs and kepyth us in hym. And the depe wysdome of þe trynyte is our moder, in whom we be closyd. And the hye goodnesse of the trynyte is our lord and in hym we be closyd and he in vs. We be closyd in the fader, and we be closyd in the son, and we are closyd in the holy gost. And the fader is beclosyd in vs, the son is beclosyd in vs, and the holy gost is beclosyd in vs, all myght, alle wysdom and alle goodnesse, one god, one lord. (20-27)

Through repetition, inversion, and a lulling rhythm, Julian of Norwich was including her readers in her own warmth which in turn was the warmth she received from His embrace.

The concept of God as mother roots in earliest Christianity and can be traced back to the Old Testament, where we find the image of the flock being looked after.[1] In the New Testament, Jesus repeatedly compared himself to a hen protecting all her chickens under her wings. The devotion to God as mother was made familiar by St. Anselm. Julian of Norwich may or may not have known his doctrine, but the concept would have appealed to her. I have shown that the need for this perception may have originated in her early youth. In her extensive preoccupation with the subject, the finely honed presentation of her insights surpassed any of the previously existing texts considering God as mother.

A.M. Allchin cites the tender way in which she described maternal feelings in connection with the motherhood of God as proof that she must have had a warm mother relationship: "Freud and Klein were not the first to observe the importance of the child's very first contacts with the mother. We can only speculate about Julian's relationship with her own mother, but it is impossible not to feel that it must have been an exceptionally satisfying one".[2] In my opinion this assumption stands on shaky ground. The extent to which the notion of God as Mother permeates her text suggests a need so deep that it might indicate unfulfilled love in her own childhood. In the light of modern psychology, it is more likely that Julian of Norwich's

---

[1] "He shall gather the lambs with his arm, and carry them in his bosom." Isaiah, 40:11.

[2] A.M. Allchin, "Julian of Norwich and the Continuity of Tradition," *The Medieval Mystical Tradition in England,* ed. Marion Glasscoe (Exeter: University of Exeter, 1980) p 83.

preoccupation with the mother-figure stemmed from inadequate love in her own life.[1] Whatever the cause for her interpretations, in her teaching, she embraced the idea and all its warmth.

(v)   Felix Culpa - The Grace of Sin[2]
I have already dealt to some extent with the importance of sin to Julian of Norwich. In her *Revelations* she occupied herself with this problem extensively, calling it "the sharpest scorge þat ony chosyn soule may be smyttyn with" (chap 39: 1-2). Yet, secure in her conviction that all would be well, she was able to speak confidently of ultimate forgiveness: "And of hys gret curtesy he doth away alle oure blame, and beholdeth vs with ruth and pytte, as children innocens and vnlothfulle." (chap 28: 33-35) Her doctrine insisted that sin, standing between man and God, was everything that was not good. In the end, however, she "saw nott synne, for ... it had no manner of substance, ne no part of beyng, ne it myght not be knowen but by the payne that is caused therof" (chap 27: 26-28). And in the same chapter: "It is tru that synne is cause of alle thys payne, but alle shalle be wele, and alle maner of thyng shalle be wele" (33-34). She considered sin as inevitable, fulfilling its purpose by making men see their own wretchedness: "for yf we felle nott, we shulde nott knowe how febyll and how wrechyd we be of oure selfe, nor also we shulde not so fulsomely know þe mervelous loue of oure maker" (chap 61: 19-21). For Julian of Norwich, sin was not the cause for eternal damnation but rather the cause for salvation. A possible conclusion could be that the more you sin, the more you will be

---

[1]   Sonja Rüttner-Cova, personal interview, June 1989.

[2]   Missal: O felix culpa, quae talem ac tantum meruit habere Redemptorem. (Exultet on Holy Saturday)

forgiven. Yet, Julian of Norwich warned against the idea that the more a man sinned the higher his exaltation would be:

> But now because of alle thys gostly comfort that is before seyde, if any man or woman be steryd by foly to sey or to thynke: if this be tru, than were it good for to synne to haue the more mede, or elles to charge the lesse to synne, beware of this steryng. For truly if it come, it is vntrue and of the enemy. (chap 40: 25-30)

In clear contradiction to the teachings of the church, she was told in her visions that sin, punishment in itself, was "behouely" (chap 27: 13). Without the opportunity of falling from grace, man would be deprived of the blessing of forgiveness. Only through being forgiven can man realize and completely experience the bliss of the love of God for humankind. By insisting on this perception, her teaching is as convincing to her readers as it is appealing. Sin belongs to God's concept of salvation, is even necessary. Whatever you do, as long as you devote your life to Him, "all will be well".[1]

(vi) Her Lasting Message

Julian of Norwich was able to sum up the fulfillment of her three wishes. The initial experience revealed a conviction that "all will be well". Keeping that in mind through her years of contemplation, she achieved a calm certainty expressed in the last paragraphs of her work.

---

[1] In chapter 51 in the scene "of a lord that hath a servant", Julian of Norwich threw further light on her attitude to sin, saying that God will reward intention, even though His children on earth may not completely fulfill their obligations.

And fro the tyme *p*at it was shewde, I desyerde oftyn tymes to wytt in what was oure lords menyng. And xv yere after and mor, I was answeryd in gostly vnderstondyng, seyeng thus: What, woldest thou wytt thy lordes menyng in this thyng? Wytt it wele, loue was his menyng. Who shewyth it the? Loue. (What shewid he the? Love.) Wherfore shewyth he it the? For loue. Holde the therin, thou shalt wytt more in the same. But thou schalt nevyr wytt therin other withoutyn ende.

Thus I lernyd, *p*at loue is oure lordes menyng. And I sawe full surely in this and in alle that or god made vs he lovyd vs, whych loue was nevyr slekyd ne nevyr shalle. And in this loue he hath done alle his werkes, and in this loue he hath made alle thynges profytable to vs, and in this loue oure lyfe is evyr lastyng. In oure makyng we had begynnyng, but the loue wher he made vs was in hym fro wyth out begynnyng. In whych loue we haue oure begynnyng, and alle this shalle we see in god with outyn ende. (chap 86: 13-27)

We see here her favourite technique of alternating her paragraphs of interpretation with passages of either description or, as here, of rhetorical questions. In lines 5-8 of the quotation we find four questions linked by rhythm, alliteration and, in her answers, repetition of her fundamental message: "Love". This repetition continues in her second paragraph of analysis. In its eleven lines, "love" (or "lovyd") is reiterated eight times. This chanting, reminiscent of the Psalms and in the style of eastern worship, evokes a sense of mystery which combines practical teaching with ecstasy. Both paragraphs end with the phrase "withoutyn ende". What is in itself a stylistic device, is made into a convincing message of her principle.

Julian of Norwich, recipient of generations of appraisal and examination, deserves her undisputed reputation. The passages I have quoted demonstrate her prowess as a gifted writer, a persuasive teacher, and an intelligent woman, an "art [that] reflects the strength of her commitment to communicate" (von Nolcken, p 101). While she was able to select from traditional, literary, and doctrinal sources, accepting some and waiving others, her only deviation from the established role of a woman was that she wrote down her experiences. Her mystical conviction that "alle will be wele" called for no changes. But as for a feminist awareness, even in its early stages of development, my enquiries have found no trace of it in her writings.

III MYSTICISM

This paper does not investigate whether Julian of Norwich was a true mystic or whether Margery Kempe deserves the title at all. But, as mystical experiences were of prime importance for both women, a short outline of the phenomenon might be helpful. Information on the subject can be found in a multitude of sources. In my summary account of mysticism I have endeavoured I mainly follow Evelyn Underhill, David Knowles, Eric Colledge, and Paul Szarmach.[1]

The origins of mysticism, that "science of ultimates" (Underhill p 25) are Oriental, Greek, and Christian in the Apostolic doctrine. The most important influence came to Europe from Dionysius the Areopagite, also called St. Denis or pseudo-Dionysius. He was probably a Syrian monk who wrote between the years 475 and 525. In England, his thoughts were first represented in the anonymous *Cloud of Unknowing* and they nourished spiritual intuitions of men from the ninth to the seventeenth century. His widest known idea is the concept of God as a circle without a circumference in whose center everything meets. God has His center everywhere, but His circumference nowhere. God is the absolutely transcendent One. All else emanates from Him. Mystical experience is achieved after shedding all forms of human knowledge until only the Absolute remains.

---

[1] David Knowles, *The English Mystical Tradition* (London: Methuen, 1961)

Eric Colledge, *The Mediaeval Mystics of England* (London: John Murray, 1962)

Paul Szarmach, *Introduction to the Medieval Mystics of Europe* (Albany: The State University of New York Press, 1984)

Julian of Norwich applied these fundamental ideas to her thinking. This understanding is mirrored in the *Revelations*: "And after this I saw god in a poynte, that is to say in my vndyrstandyng, by which syght I saw that he is in althyng." (chap 11: 3-4)

Mysticism, what Evelyn Underhill also terms "ultimate Reality" (p 72), seems to represent the essence of man's religious experience; and mystics, again according to Evelyn Underhill, are heroic examples of the life of spirit. J.H. Leuba points out that one mark of a genuine mystic is a heroic spirit with which he tenaciously pursues a definite moral ideal.[1]

Mystics are not concerned with improving anything in the visible universe. A true mystic, whose heart is always set on the One - the personal and living object of love - is preoccupied with the transcendental. The goal of mystic experience is the development of the "power of apprehending the Absolute, Pure Being, the utterly Transcendent" (Underhill p 36). "The business and method of mysticism is love" (Underhill p 85). By passing through consecutive levels in mystical progress, the seeker may fulfill his yearning - Union with the Absolute. These stages are all on God's terms, and if He so wishes.

The first step is the awakening of the Self, which is usually accompanied by exaltation. The second is the phase of purgation, a stage of pain and effort. The third, which can be the final stage, is the phase of illumination. The fourth step is a "dark night of the soul" (Underhill p 121), often perceived to be the absence of God, an experience felt to be especially brutal after the preceding illumination. The fifth and last phase is the goal of any true mystic: "oned with bliss" as Evelyn Underhill (p 68) calls it; the state of Union, of perfect knowledge, of complete understanding.

---

[1]   James H. Leuba, *The Psychology of Religious Mysticism* (London: AMS, 1925)

In the mystic state, the Absolute, that complete reality, is touched. This living union with the One is achieved in a latent form of consciousness. The final illumination is the knowledge of God, a condition incorporated into modern psychology in the doctrine of the unconscious or subliminal personality with its range of psychic life below and beyond the conscious field.

In contemplation, the mystic can go from one level of consciousness to the next, thus liberating a deeper and deeper perception. The object of contemplation can be almost anything one can concentrate on. A hazelnut in her hand led Julian of Norwich to a fundamental understanding of creation.

All mystics insist that the key to mystic experience - the apprehension of the Absolute - is a "spark".
Neither Julian of Norwich nor Margery Kempe made explicit reference to this idea, however, it re-emerges in the Quakers' concept of the inner light.

Since mysticism is the only channel of communication with the spiritual world contemplation, for the mystic, is a psychic gateway. However, not all who experience trance, ecstasy, vision or other similar phenomena can be termed mystic. Underhill stresses the importance of disentangling "psycho-physical accidents" from mystical experience.

While the Absolute of the metaphysicians remains a diagram, the Absolute of the mystics is lovable and can be experienced. Mystics cast off the ties of the senses and become one with the All. What seems to be passivity is actually a state of the most intense activity. Walter Hilton calls this state "restful travail" or "holy idleness".

In the true mystical state the fully developed and completely conscious soul can feel the Infinite above all reason and knowledge. This experience can be both life- enhancing and healing. Mysticism implies the abolition of individuality. It is a movement of the heart trying to surrender to the ultimate reality.

The mediaeval mystic, exhibiting the richness of unitive life, was supported by traditional dogma and readily accepted. The mediaeval age was more conducive to mysticism than our own. However, mystical experience has often found expression in art. Thus, the prose writers (of fourteenth century England) like Richard Rolle of Hampole and the unknown author of *The Cloud of Unknowing*; the poetry of metaphysicals such as Herbert (1593-1633); the watercolour illustrations for the Book of Job by William Blake (1757-1827), and the music of Ralph Vaughan Williams (1872-1958) to the same theme, enable us to trace the phenomenon to the twentieth century.

While one might expect present times to be less sympathetic to meditative forms of worship, the current interest in eastern philosophies indicates that mysticism is alive today.

IV MARGERY KEMPE

The text of *The Book of Margery Kempe* is in three parts:
- i   The Proem
- ii Book I   87 chapters
- iii Book II   10 chapters; prayers of the creature[1]

a) Textual History of the *Book of Margery Kempe*

The first record of Margery Kempe's work dates back to 1501 when selected passages from her *Book* were published by Wynkyn de Worde in a seven-page quarto pamphlet entitled: "A shorte treatyse of contemplacyon taught by our lorde Ihesu cryste, or taken out of the boke of Margerie kempe of lynn". The only known copy is in the Cambridge University Library.

The editor seems to have taken great care not to offend any religious sensitivity. Nineteen passages were presented irrespective of their original position in the *Book*. Every reference to Margery Kempe's actual life was omitted. The result was a text that left the reader without any idea of the tantalizing and intriguing character of the author.

In 1521 Henry Pepwell published a volume containing seven mystical English texts. The edition by Wynkyn de Worde was included unchanged. The misleading information that Margery Kempe was a "devoute ancres" was first put out by Pepwell. Sanford Brown-Meech, the editor of the Butler-Bowden MS, sees this erroneous claim as the result of the biased selection of texts in the Wynkyn de Worde edition.

---

[1] Unless specified, chapter numbers refer to Book I. Where I have quoted from the proem or from Book II, I have noted the fact. All quotations are from the Butler-Bowden MS, edited by Sanford Brown Meech and Hope Emily Allen.

After 1521 no trace of Margery Kempe or the *Book* appeared until 1934, when a manuscript of the *Book* was found in the library of Colonel William Erdeswick Ignatius Butler-Bowden. Subsequently, the American scholar, Hope Emily Allen, identified the text.

By analyzing the quality of the leaves, experts have found this manuscript to have been written before rather than after 1450.

b)   Margery Kempe, "*þ*is creatur"

The only extant contemporary source of biographical detail is her own *Book*, supplemented by historical registers in Norfolk.

The author of *The Book of Margery Kempe* was born around 1373 in Bishop's Lynn, a bustling market town on the river Ouse in Norfolk, known today as King's Lynn.

She came from a prosperous family. Town records identify her as the daughter of John Brunham, several times mayor and alderman of the "hey Gylde of *þe* Trinyte in N.". At about twenty she was married to the well-meaning but less successful John Kempe, whose debts are mentioned in various passages of her book. Still, she described him as "euyir hauying tendyrnes & compassyon of hir" (chap 1).[1] Some information on her background can be found in chapter 46 of the *Book*. Accused of Lollardy, imprisoned, and questioned by the mayor of Leicester (probably around 1416), she told him:

> Syr, I am of Lynne in Norfolke, a good mannys dowtyr of *þe* same Lynne, whech hath ben meyr fyve tymes of *þ*at worshepful burwgh and aldyrman also

---

[1] The person of John Kempe will be discussed in more depth when dealing with Margery Kempe's creating of her own private sphere.

many yerys, & I haue a good man, also a burgeys of *þe* seyd town, Lynne, to myn husbond.

Her illiteracy might seem surprising, for the emerging merchant class was very conscious of the importance of education, as is evidenced by the increasing number of schools in the fifteenth century.

> Municipal guilds and individual burghers and merchants, increasing in wealth and in family connections with the landed gentry, took pride in founding schools which would give to other boys of their town or shire a chance to rise, either to be future priests and bishops, or equally well to be future Mayors, merchants, royal ministers and clerks, judges, lawyers, gentry capable of managing their estates and ruling their country for the King.[1]

Yet this growth in education did not include girls - Margery Kempe had to depend on scribes when she told her story.

After a difficult pregnancy and the traumatic birth of the first of the fourteen children that she carried to term she became very ill. She thought she was going to die and called for her confessor "for sche had a thyng in conscyens whech sche had neuyr schewyd be-forn *þ*at tyme in alle her lyfe" (chap 1). But when it came to confessing this particular sin she felt unable to do so. Actually this sin, conceivably just a slight misdemeanor, was never disclosed. For fear of eternal damnation she went out of her mind and, for "half yer viij wekys & odde days" (chap 1) fell into what could be called a "black night of the soul". Although Evelyn Underhill uses the identical phrase to describe

---

[1] G.M. Trevelyan, *Illustrated Social History*, vol 2 (London: The Reprint Society, 1963) p 70.

the fourth stage of a mystic's progress towards perfection, in the case of Margery Kempe at this point, her condition can most probably be diagnosed as postpartum depression.[1] Her condition manifested itself in visions of devils telling her to forsake her faith, kill her family, and direct her wretched violence against herself.[2]

The appearance of Jesus in the shape of a man brought about a miraculous and complete recovery.

> And a-noon þe creature was stabelyd in hir wyttys & in hir reson as wel as evyr sche was be-forn, and preyd hir husbond as so soon as he cam to hir þat sche myght haue þe keys of þe botery to takyn hir mete & drynke as sche had don be-forn. (chap 1)

After this return to health she felt bound to become God's servant and do penance though she did not mitigate her pride. Her attempts to make money through business ventures proved disastrous. She saw these failures as God's scourges chastising her for her sins and she began to concentrate on the way of everlasting life.

After twenty years of adventurous pilgrimages she returned home in 1431 to care for her sick husband. She did this with joy, remembering the good times they had had together. At this time she started dictating her *Book*.

A last reference to her occurs in documents mentioning the admission of Margery Kempe into the Trinity Guild of Lynn in 1438 and 1439.

---

[1] William B. Ober, "Margery Kempe: Hysteria and Mysticism Reconciled," *Psychiatry and Literature* IV(1985): pp 24-40.

[2] It is interesting to note that this is the only time her mother is mentioned: "..sche schuld forsake...hyr fadyr, hyr modyr, & alle hire frendys." (chap 1)

The Book of Margery Kempe is the testimonial of a woman living in the world trying to lead a contemplative life. It is a record of the trials she went through in order to be able to live this chosen life - a life of chastity, prayer and desire for God; of travels to holy places; of compassion for her fellows; of emotional outbreaks in the form of uncontrollable fits of weeping and shrieking. Most important though, it traces the defining of her own personality by means available to her and acceptable to fifteenth century mores.

She had as her monitor Jesus, who assured her that he would never forsake her:

> For, whan þow gost to chyrch, I go wyth þe; whan þu syttest at þi mete, I sytte wyth þe; whan þu gost to þi bed, I go wyth þe; whan þu gost owt of towne, I go wyth þe. I far sum-tyme wyth my grace to þe as I do wyth þe sunne. Sum-tyme þow wetyst wel þe sunne schynyth al abrod þat many man may se it, & sum-tyme it is hyd vndyr a clowde þat men may not se it, & ȝet is þe sunne neuyr þe lesse in hys hete ne in hys brytnesse. And ryght so far I be þe & be my chosen sowlys. (chap 14)

Thus strengthened, she was able to overcome difficulties and temptations, and defend her innocence.

It was her highest goal to serve the Lord, yet she also had a family to look after. Since a retreat as a recluse was out of the question, she took the only option available and followed the example of women mystics like Bridget of Sweden, Dorothea of Pomerania, Dorothea of Monthau, and Marie d'Oignies. All had been married and Margery Kempe was probably familiar with their lives, having heard their stories, perhaps on her travels in

Europe.[1] We know from her own admission that she was interested in writings of other English mystics and had had texts by Richard Rolle (chaps 17 and 28) and Walter Hilton (chaps 17 and 58) read to her.

Unlike Julian of Norwich, she did not write the *Book* in order to teach. She wrote because God told her to do so and because she wanted her achievements to be known.

However, as in the work of Julian of Norwich, the content and style of Margery Kempe's text reflect contemporary background and environment. The digest of impressions of a life as the daughter of a politician and merchant, the business ventures, the pregnancies together with a highly emotional and compassionate character and apparently astounding powers of recall, schooled by oral learning, make *The Book of Margery Kempe* a valuable and fascinating testimony in the history of women's liberation.

In comparison with Julian of Norwich she must always be considered the lesser of the two as long as religious, historical, and literary criteria - expectations "fathered by masculine consciousness" - are applied.[2] As soon as we free her from patronizing modes of criticism, we begin to see her as the person she was, colourful and independent.

---

[1] "Seynt Brydys boke" is actually mentioned in chapters 17 and 58.

[2] Adrienne Rich, *Blood, Bread and Poetry*. Selected Prose 1979-1985. (London: Virago, 1987) p 7.

c) The *Book* and Margery Kempe

Our knowledge of Margery Kempe is the *Book*. Much late twentieth century opinion calls the text the first autobiography in English, but book titles like *The Apprentice Saint* of Louise Collis show no more than a benevolent condescension towards Margery Kempe's aspirations.[1] Furthermore, Susan Dickman[2] points out that she has been identified "as a neurotic housewife whose spirituality, though derived from conventional sources, was designed to solve her personal problems" and an "out-and-out hysteric" (p 151). Edmund Colledge and James Walsh refer to her "morbid self-engrossment" (p 39), and Anthony Goodman[3] went so far as to call Margery Kempe an "anti-social virus ... viewed with irritation and distrust" (p 356).

My first effort at reading confirmed both reputations. However, to elicit a traditionally chronological biography of its author from the *Book*, I had to glean straws of information from apparently random sections. Margery Kempe's ordering was not sequential, and it was not until I abandoned chronology that I was able to see both woman and text in a new light. Rather than the narrative of a life, *The Book of Margery Kempe* is the record of a struggle. Continued analysis made the literary importance of the *Book* recede while the personal achievements of its author assumed paramount importance. Yet it is only through her record that we meet Margery Kempe.

---

[1] Louise Collis, *The Apprentice Saint* (London: Michael Joseph, 1964)

[2] Susan Dickman, "Margery Kempe and the Continental Tradition of the Pious Woman," *Medieval Mystical Tradition in England.* Dartington 1984, ed. Marion Glasscoe (Cambridge: D.S. Brewer, 1984)

[3] Anthony E. Goodman, "The piety of John Brunham's daughter of Lynn," *Medieval Women.* ed. Derek Baker (Oxford: Basil Blackwell, 1978) p 365.

(i)   The *Book* as Literature

Close study of the style of *The Book of Margery Kempe* might seem unrewarding. She used scribes; her rambling, colloquial expression may have been altered or at least influenced to some unknown extent. But the order of the incidents she described, the figures of speech, are most probably her very own. Her prose sounds spoken rather than written, offering itself to the confessor rather than the literary critic. In her essay on the style of Richard Rolle, Rita Copeland summarized Cicero's words: "This insistence upon the correlation between subject matter and style - defined as decorum - is the foundation of any treatment of style itself" (p 57). Such analysis would be a barren exercise if directed at *The Book*, in which the author aspired to record rather than achieve 'decorum'.

She struggled with the same problem that we already know from Julian of Norwich: expressing the confusingly inexpressible. Margery Kempe described

> how sum-tyme *þ*e Fadyr of Hevyn dalyd to hir sowle as pleynly and as veryly as o [sic] frend spekyth to a-no*þ*er be bodyly spech; sum-tyme *þ*e Secunde Persone in Trinyte; sum-tyme alle thre Personys in Trinyte & o substawns in Godhede dalyid to hir sowle & informyd hir in hir feyth & in hys lofe how sche xuld lofe hym, worshepyn hym, & dredyn hym, so excellently *þ*at sche herd neuyr boke, ne*þ*y*r* Hyltons boke, ne Bridis boke, ne Stimulus Amoris, ne Incendium Amoris, ne non o*þ*er *þ*at euyr sche herd redyn *þ*at spak so hyly of lofe of God but *þ*at sche felt werkyng in hir sowle yf sche cowd or ellys myght a schewyd as sche felt. (chap 17)

58

That she was unable to write and read does not mean she could not have had the scribe read back her dictation. We know she had a remarkably eidetic memory so she was certainly able to check the content and make sure his words expressed her meaning. "& so he red it ouyr be-forn *þ*is creatur euery word, sche sum-tyme helpyng where ony difficulte was" (proem). Her powers of recall are illustrated where she attempted a verbatim report of a conversation held, many years earlier, in Italy, a country whose language she had not learnt. The Italian woman asked: "Margerya in pouerte?" And Margery Kempe, "understondyng what pe lady ment, seyd a-3en, '3a, grawnt pouerte, Madam' " (chap 38).

Passages that testify to the fact that she did edit her text are found at the end of chapter 17, where the reader is instructed to study chapter 21 before going on; and in chapter 60, where the author referrred to a priest whom she pointed out she had mentioned before. Also she frequently used the phrase "as is beforn-wretyn" (e.g. *Book*, chap 4; *Book* II, chap 8)

One of the fascinating aspects of the *Book* is that it includes elements peculiar to several literary genres. Frances and Joseph Gies go so far as to call Margery Kempe "the author of the first biography, and first autobiography, in English."[1] To accept the first of their claims one would have to disregard Anglo-Saxon literature with its wealth of "Lives of Saints" and secular biography such as Aelfric's "Life of King Oswald". While one does quibble with the epithet "first", its third person narrative qualifies it to be designated as biography. The most obvious term to apply would be that of the religious autobiography, even though the convention had not been defined

---

[1] Frances Gies and Joseph Gies, *Women in the Middle Ages*. (New York: Barnes and Noble, 1978)

in the fifteenth century. However, unlike regular autobiographies, the *Book* does not begin with the birth or childhood of the author. In her proem, Margery Kempe described the difficulties she encountered in actually getting her *Book* written. Because she called her efforts "labowr", scholars such as Marlena Corcoran have equated the birth of the *Book* with the birth of a beloved child, implying that where an autobiography would deal first with the writer's early years, Margery Kempe concerned herself with her "child's" beginning.[1] Tempting as this theory may be, her other uses of "labour" are less specific. In chapter 8 of *Book* II, e.g., where her companions permitted her to travel with them only if she could match their speed. "So sche folwyd aftyr hem wyth gret labowr tyl *þ*ei comyn at a good town..." And in chapter 7 too, when pilgrims hearing about "*þe* creaturys labowr" accepted her as their fellow traveller. Labour simply stands for very hard work, as indeed giving birth, particularly under mediaeval conditions, is.

Before I deal at greater length with the *Book* as a biography, let me consider other genres it could be assigned to.

It is also a travel book. Memoir would be a possible definition because the work depends on recall and because the work is focused on its author.

One thing it is not is a diary. *The Book* is no day to day account with day to day reactions such as anger at her fellow travellers or disappointment with her own inadequacies. Though set in a religious not literary frame, everything described was seen from her highly personal point of view. However, a regular diary would record emotions, but Margery Kempe's text reflects

---

[1] Marlena G. Corcoran, "The Foresaid Creature". The Construction of the Subject in "*The Book of Margery Kempe,*". paper. n. d.

the calmness of recollection. We only encounter rapture where she is dealing with the divine.

The rather scanty definition of "novel", what J.A. Cuddon[1] calls "the hold-all and Gladstone bag of literature", in the Oxford Advanced Learner's Dictionary: "story in prose, long enough to fill one or more volumes, about either imaginary or historical people", can very loosely be applied to Margery Kempe's work. However, there is no proper plot or chronological ordering of narrative.

We are inclined to categorize literary works. However, applying such analysis to pre-Renaissance literature must often define what the works are not. This is particularly the case when dealing with *The Book of Margery Kempe*. She herself anticipated this criticism:

> Thys boke is not wretyn in ordyr, euery thyng aftyr oþer as it wer don, but lych as þe mater cam to þe creatur in mend whan it schuld be wretyn, for it was so long er it was wretyn þat sche had for-getyn þe tyme & þe ordyr whan thyngys befellyn. (proem)

The *Book*, like many mediaeval homilies, plays and texts, abounds in images. It is surely impossible to state with certainty which figures are derived and which original. For example, Margery Kempe, like Julian of Norwich, made expressive use of the stylistic devices of
and repetition. Studies of much earlier sermons and texts in the homiletic tradition prove that these customs were in practice from the beginning of recorded literature. Apart from the rhetorical aspect of lending a definitely rhythmic touch to a text, enumeration and repetition helped to stress the importance of

---

[1] J.A. Cuddon. *A Dictionary of Literary Terms* (London: Penguin, 1979) p 431.

what was being said, and also served both speaker and listener as a reminder of the wording of the presentation.

As mentioned above (p 59), she was familiar with "Seynt Brydys boke". Her mentioning Rolle and Hilton shows that she knew other contemporary mystical texts. Hope Emily Allen suggests that she may have already admired this vivid image in Rolle's *Meditations on the Passion* when she likened the body of Christ to a dove-cote in chapter 28, "mor ful of wowndys þan euyr was duffehows of holys" (p 291-292). On the other hand, pigeons belonged to any mediaeval city and since her personality would have allowed for such dramatic reality she could have coined the expression herself. The author of the *Book* may actually have been present at a performance of miracle plays. In *Noah and His Wife, The Flood and Its Waning*[1] from the York Cycle of miracle plays, for instance, the tender yet important scene of the dove would have appealed to Margery Kempe. The image of this bird appears again in chapter 20:

> On a day þis creatur was heryng hir Messe, a ȝong man and a good prest heldyng up þe Sacrament in hys handys ouyr hys hed, þe Sacrament schok & flekeryd to & fro as a dowe flekeryth wyth hir wengys.

Dramatized Bible stories were performed as early as the thirteenth century. B. A. Windeatt, the translator of *The Book of Margery Kempe*, points out that Margery Kempe's dreadfully realistic representation of the crucifixion in chapter 80 closely resembles passages from the "Wakefield Mystery Play of the

---

[1] Thomas J. Garbàty, ed., *Medieval English Literature*. (Lexington, MA: Heath, 1984).

Scourging" and the "York Crucifixion Play" (p 326).

Though one can appreciate Margery Kempe's pictorial language, no claim for either originality or adherence to a literary pattern can be made here because she was not aware of literary tradition. Rather than focus on the minutiae of stylistic analysis then, we can study her text as an expression of the author's personality, vision, and experience, hoping to elicit a more distinct portrayal that will enable us to say, "this is Margery Kempe".

(ii) The *Book* as a Biography

As was mentioned before, this text is often reminiscent of aural confession, full of non sequiturs: the ramblings of an old person, bringing back past times, perhaps forgetting the actual order of things, but on the other hand able to see sequences much more clearly in restrospect. "The manner of the prose is that of storytelling" (Corcoran p 3). Thus the selection of incidents she considered worth recording is of importance in an interpretation of her writing, as well as her choice of words and stylistic devices

Her background, her unusual life, her amazing character, her stubbornness, her stamina, her aggravating behaviour in public, her ability to make use of what was available - all these are reflected in the text.

Though sometimes keenly aware of other people, she could also be totally oblivious of their feelings. For instance, she was hurt when some of her fellow travellers, unwilling to go on in her company, muttered behind her back, yet she did not seem to connect their behaviour with her own conduct.

William Provost suggests the possibility of Margery's being a fraud, because none of her "dalliances" were held in dreams. Yet he has to admit that, given the authenticity of the *Book*, Margery Kempe must have been a powerful, honest person who spent her life with unwavering energy actively testifying to Christian principles of love by living them.[1]

Wolfgang Riehle cites her as a good example of the late phase of the development of affective devotion (*The Middle English Mystics* p 11).

Margery Kempe was in constant communication with the Lord Jesus, the Father, and any number of Saints.

> Sym-tyme owr Lady spak to hir and comforted hir ... Sumtyme Seynt Peter, er Seynt Powle, sumtyme Seynt Mary Mawdelyn, Seynt Katheryne, Seynt Margaret, er what seynt in Heuyn *p*at sche cowde thynke on thorw *p*e wil & sufferawns of God, *p*ei spokyn to *p*e vndyrstondyng of hir sowle.... (chap 87)

They appeared to her and she frequently described herself participating actively in scenes from the Bible. In one of her meditations she became the nurse of Mary and was later present at the birth of Jesus. In her meditations, she witnessed the Epiphany, accompanied the Holy Family into Egypt, and was present at many scenes of the Passion.

As I have pointed out, the author of the Book almost certainly had no scholastic training. While on the one hand this made her dependent on scribes, on the other hand it presents us with a spontaneously naive text. The question of why the Book

---

[1] William Provost, "The Religious Enthusiast: Margery Kempe," *Medieval Woman Writers*, ed. Katharina M. Wilson (Atlanta: University of Georgia Press, 1984)

was written in the third person singular has not yet been answered satisfactorily. It has been suggested that the author did not want to appear as the subject of a book. I tend to disagree with this argument. Margery Kempe was independent enough to travel to the Holy Land on her own, to defend herself successfully against powerful adversaries. She seemed very much aware of her own importance as a person. That she should suddenly want to be unobtrusive seems to be conflicting with her character. In my opinion the use of the third person singular could very well be due to the scribes, especially during the rewriting of the first manuscript. In eastern mysticism, where the mystic is distinctly defined as a medium, the use of the third person singular in recording divine experiences is the accepted form.

Margery Kempe's interpretation of her experiences was subjected to only the most general contemporary religious thinking, spread by word of mouth, and thus based wholly on the culture she lived in. Her own unadulterated personality and her very own experiences before she turned to the Lord are therefore the starting point for whatever approach we choose. If we are prepared to accept the Book as the first autobiography, since there were no patterns to imitate, by what criteria should it be reviewed? We have to keep in mind that, though it survived in written form, the Book was in fact spoken by the author. In this sense it is not unlike books such as Peig Sayers' *An Old Woman's Reflection* and Naomi Mitchison's *You May Well Ask*, reflecting a current interest in collecting oral documents.[1] This aspect adds to the importance of the Book.

---

[1] Naomi Mitchison, *You May Well Ask* (London: Victor Gollancz, 1979)

Peig Sayers, *An Old Woman's Reflection* (Oxford: Oxford University Press, 1968)

Paradoxically, we can only hope to make a valid appraisal of Margery Kempe's text in the terms she dictates, for the only source for her character analysis is her very text.

In order to deal with Margery Kempe, the mystic, therefore, some sort of summary of her story seems essential. Just as categorizing her Book into definable literary genres has proved impossible, so attempting a lucid resumé is doomed to fail. Margery Kempe appeared indifferent to chronology and her recall as an old woman was conditioned by her spiritual aims. In any one chapter, what she selected for recording was relevant to her divine way.

I have quoted extensively in order to convey the tantalizing immediacy of the text. Furthermore, the passages chosen draw the reader's attention to the confused ordering of her reminiscences.

(iii)   Margery Kempe's Story in Developmental Sequence
Having been severely ill for a number of months, Margery Kempe was cured magically by the appearance of Jesus in the shape of a beautiful young man "most semly, most bewtyouws, & most amyable, þat euyr myght be seen wyth mannys eye, clad in a mantyl of purpyl sylke" (chap 1). After her miraculous recovery she turned to the Lord, did penance, prayed, and was shriven many times but did not leave her worldly ways. She still loved being admired:

> Neuyr-þe-lesse, sche wold not leeyn hir pride ne hir pompows aray þat sche had usyd be-forn-tym, neiþyr for hyr husbond ne for noon oþer mannys cownsel. And yet sche wyst ful wel þat men seyden hir ful mech velany, for sche weryd gold pypys on hir hevyd & hir hodys wyth þe typettys were

66

daggyd. Hir clokys also wer daggyd & leyd wyth dyuers colowrs be-tween þe daggys þat it schuld be þe mor staryng to mennys syght and her-self þe mor ben worshepd. (chap 2)

She turned against her husband:

> And, whan hir husbond wold speke to hir for to leuyn hir pride, sche answeeryd schrewdly & schortly & seyd þat sche was comyn of worthy kenred, - hym semyd neuyr for to a weddyd hir, for hir fadyr was sum-tyme meyr of þe town N., and sythyn he was alderman of þe hey Gylde of þe Trinyte in N. And þerfor sche wold sauyn þe whorschyp of hir kynred what-so-euyr ony man seyd. (chap 2)

"And than, for pure coveytyse & for to maynten hir pride, sche gan to brewyn & was on of þe grettest brewers in the town N. a iij ȝer or iiij" (chap 2) until her ventures failed:

> ...whan þe ale was fayr standyng undyr berm as any man myght se, sodenly þe berm wold fallyn down þat alle þe ale was lost euery brewyng aftyr oþer, þat hir seruawntys weryn a-schamyd & wold not dwellyn wyth hir. (chap 2)

She "be-thowt hir of a newe huswyfre" (chap 2) and tried her hand at milling. However, the horses turned stubborn and refused to pull, despite the efforts of their handler, who in turn left her service. She found herself abandoned and

> it was noysed a-bowt *þe* town of N. *þ*at *þ*er wold ne *þ*yr man ne best don seruyse to *þ*e seyd creatur, *þ*an summe seyden sche was a-cursyd; sum seyden God toke opyn veniawns up-on hir. (chap 2)

She interpreted these failures as God's punishment:

> *þ*an sche askyd God mercy & forsoke hir pride, hir coueytyse, & desyr *þ*at sche had of *þ*e worshepys of *þ*e world, & dede grett bodyly penawnce, & gan to entyr *þ*e wey of euyr-lestyng lyfe, as schal be seyd aftyr. (chap 2)

One night in bed with her husband, hearing heavenly music, she jumped up and cried: "Alas, *þ*at euyr I dede synne, it is ful mery in Hevyn" (chap 3). The music was so sweet that whenever she thought about it afterwards, or when anything reminded her of it she began to sob and cry. This "gift of tears", common to a number of continental mystics such as Mary of Oignies, who is referred to by the author in chapter 62, was not to leave her for the greater part of her life. These weeping fits were to bring her many difficulties yet, unexpectedly, seemed a source of satisfaction:

> sche was sumtyme so bareyn fro teerys a day er sumtyme half a day & had so gret peyne for desyr *þ*at sche wold a 3ouyn al *þ*is worlde, 3yf it had ben hir, for a fewe teerys, er a suffyrd ryth gret bodily peyne for to gotyn hem wyth. And *þ*an, whan sche was so bareyn, sche cowde fynde no joye ne no comforte in mete ne drynke ne dalyawns but euyr was heuy in cher & in cuntenawnce tyl God wolde send hem to hir a-geyn, & *þ*an was sche mery a-now. (chap 82)

She began to turn away from her previous life, did penance, fasted and spent a lot of time in church, in meditation, and private prayer. Her desire for sexual contact with her husband left her completely:

> And aftyr *þ*is tyme sche had neuyr desyr to komown fleschly wyth hyre husbonde, for *þ*e dette of matrimony was so abhominabyl to hir *þ*at sche had leuar, hir thowt, etyn or drynkyn *þ*e wose, *þ*e mukke in *þ*e chanel, *þ*an to consentyn to any fleschly comownyng saf only for obedyens. (chap 3)

At this time her wish for a chaste life first took shape. I consider this the beginning of her fight for independence: freeing herself by demanding the right to her own body. Her husband would not agree to her desire, though, and she suffered: "He wold haue hys wylle, & sche obeyd wyth greet weepyng" (chap 3).

In chapter 17, in a very important passage, she mentioned that after the birth of yet another child, Jesus told her not to have any more children. I maintain that most of the heavenly orders she received were transmutations of her own fervent wishes. After fourteen births, a yearning for the cessation of the breeding process is more than understandable. Given the duties of a woman at the time, such a wish could, for obvious reasons, never be uttered. Chastity, however, would lead to the desired result. If Margery Kempe's position as a married woman made her idea somewhat awkward, her pursuing the goal to please the Lord would obviate any objection to chastity. By embracing the heavenly way she made her choice unexceptionable.

I suppose we may assume that her own sexuality, which she sought to suppress, remained a problem to her. When she thought that all bodily lusts had been quenched, and when she certainly had no wish for intercourse with her husband, she was greatly distressed by her sudden desire to make love to the stranger who had propositioned her. However, the man himself declined in the end, and to her this meant that he had only been sent to test her (chap 4). She was also tormented by dreams of men exposing themselves for her viewing. The devil forced her to choose which one she wanted to prostitute herself with first (chap 59). These examples of suppressed sexuality certainly suggest that she was struggling to come to terms with the physical needs conflicting with the accepted idea of saintliness.

How deeply she was traumatized by the issue of sexuality can be seen in the unabated fear of rape that was to haunt her for the rest of her life.

> And on nyghtys had sche most dreed oftyn-tymys, & peradventur it was of hir gostly enmy, for sche was euyr a-ferd to be rauischyd er defilyd. Sche durst trustyn on no man; whedir sche had cawse er non, sche was euyr a-ferd. Sche durst ful euyl slepyn any nyth, for sche wend men wolde defylyd hir. (*Book* II, chap 7)

In order to do more penance for her sins, only one of which was lechery, she, unnoticed by her husband, began to wear a hairshirt day and night. Whenever in company she talked about the saintliness of paradise, but since she continued having children, her neighbours, understandably, began to accuse her of hypocrisy:

> Why speke 3e so oft of þe myrth þat is in Heuen; 3e know it not & 3e haue not be þer no mor þan we," & wer wroth wyth hir for sche wold not her no speke of worldly thyngys as þei dedyn & as sche dede beforn-tyme. (chap 3)

She started going on pilgrimages, first in England, accompanied by her husband, and later to Europe on her own. Also "the great trek for all medievals", the sacred expedition to the Holy Land, she undertook alone.[1] She visited bishops, anchorites and other religious people in order to get permission for her diverse endeavours such as travelling and going to communion more often than usual.

For two years, however, she experienced spiritual strength, until "Sche was smet wyth þe dedly wownd of veynglory" (chap 4). She wanted a sign from Jesus: "...sche desyred many tymes þat þe Crucifix xuld losyn hys handys fro þe crosse & halsyn hir in tokyn of lofe" (chap 4). As a result He sent her three years of tribulation with fear of the devil and libidinous thoughts.

This proof of her weakness plunged her into despair and she was afraid that the Lord had left her. In one of her fits of weeping Jesus appeared to her, assured her of His love thus bringing this three-year phase to an end. In the same vision, Margery Kempe received precise instructions for the next step in her progress towards the heavenly way, one of which was to meditate daily after six o'clock.

This tailoring of her day to satisfy worldly and spiritual demands illustrates Margery Kempe's duality. Where her

---

[1] Valerie M. Lagorio, "Defensorium Contra Oblectratores," *Mysticism, Medieval and Modern*. Salzburg Studies in English Literature under the Direction of Professor Erwin A. Stürzl. Elizabethan and Renaissance Studies 92:20, Editor: Dr. James Hogg. Institut für Anglistik und Amerikanistik, (Salzburg:Universität Salzburg, 1986) pp 29-49.

subconscious frequently produced patterns of suffering acceptable because of her desire for penance, no divine edict was permitted to cut short a full working day. A diligent woman of her time, she would not let meditation interfere with her chores, which would presumably be over by six. Clearly, her practicality was one of the controlling factors that shaped her dream world. As a housewife used to organizing heterogeneous demands, she must have known that worldly duties would keep her busy till evening.

We have other examples of her innate practicality. For years she received tokens in the form of auditive, visual, olfactory and tactile experiences. Thus, she heard delectable music so deafening that she could not have heard a man speaking to her unless - here Margery Kempe's personality shines through - he spoke very loudly. Sometimes she heard noises that frightened her:

> On was a maner of sownde as it had ben belwys blowyng in her ere. Sche, beyng a-basshed perof, was warnyd in hir sowle no fer to haue, for it was *pe* sownd of *pe* Holy Gost. & *p*an owyr Lord turnyd *p*at sownde in-to *pe* voys of a dowe, & sithyn he turnyd into *pe* voys of a lityl bryd whech is called a reedbrest *p*at song ful merily in hir ryght ere. (chap 36)

In all her rapture she was able to notice that it was her right ear that the bird sang into!

She saw angels. But, where most religious writers reach for extravagant images, white things flying reminded Margery Kempe, who had been a miller, of moths, an everpresent problem in any granary: "Sche sey with hir bodily eyne many white thyngys flying al a-bowte hir on euery syde as thykke in a maner as motys in the sunne" (chap 35).

She smelt celestial odours and she felt the fire of love burning in her chest:

> Also owr Lord 3af hir an-o*p*er tokne, *p*e whech enduryd a-bowtyn xvj 3er & it encresyd euyr mor & mor , & *p*at was a flawme of fyer wondir hoot & delectabyl & ryth comfortabyl, nowt wastyng but euyr incresyng, of lowe, for thow *p*e wedyr wer neuyr so colde, sche felt *p*e hete brennyng in hir brest & at hir hert, as verily as a man schuld felyn *p*e material fyer 3yf he put hys hand or hys fynger perin. (chap 35)

It is tempting to envisage Margery Kempe busy cooking and burning her finger on a hot pot. Cold weather probably was a worry for the lady of the house, so the idea of any constant fire burning wherever must have been associated with contentment.

One time when she was in church a large wooden beam and a piece of rock fell down from the roof and hit her. She described with a housewife's eye for detail the size and weight of the objects:

> Sodeynly fel down from *p*e heyest party of *p*e cherch-vowte fro undyr *p*e fote of *p*e sparre on hir hed & on hir bakke a ston whech weyd iij pownd & a schort ende of a tre weyng vj pownd *p*at hir thowt hir bakke brakke a-sundyr, and sche ferd sche had be deed a lytyl whyle. Soon aftyr sche cryed 'Ihesu mercy,' a-non hir peyn was gon. (chap 9)

The Lord assured her that this was actually a miracle and that he was going to perform many more. Furthermore, Jesus assured her that He had chosen her:

> For I have ordeyned *þe* to knele be-fore *þe* Trynyte for to prey for al *þe* world, for many hundryd thowsand sowlys schal be sauyd be *þe* prayers. (chap 7)

Jesus allowed her to choose the person she wanted to have with her in heaven and she asked for her confessor rather than her father or husband because, she pointed out, she would never be able to repay her spiritual guide for his kindness to her. I would add that her confessor, bound by his vows, probably never made any physical demands upon her. This wish for her spiritual guide to be at her side in paradise rather than anyone from her worldly environment obviously exemplifies her desire to leave the mundane for the heavenly way. In spite of this ardent wish there is no evidence in the *Book* of Margery Kempe of longing for death or even for a life in retreat.

During one of her many prayers for chastity, Jesus advised her that if she abstained from both food and drink on Fridays - a condition that was to come in handy in her later deal with her husband - her wish would be granted before Whitsun. The next time her husband approached her she cried "Ihesus, help me!" (chap 9). From that moment on her husband was unable to touch her.

On a hot summer's day, while they were on the road, the question of chastity arose again between Margery Kempe and her husband. He asked her if she would rather see him slain than sleep with him and she answered: "For-so*þe* I had leuar se 3ow be slayn *þ*an we schuld turne ayen to owyr vnclennesse." His resigned answer was: "3e arn no good wyfe" (chap 11). Again she begged him to live chastely with her and he suggested that if she continued to sleep in his bed, paid his debts, and gave up her fasting on Fridays he would make a vow of chastity. She declined to give up fasting and he threatened to make love to her. She began to pray and Jesus advised her to accept the husband's offer:

> & he xal han *p*at he deseyreth. For, my derworthy dowtyr, *p*at was *p*e cawse pat I bad *p*e fastyn for *p*u schuldyst *p*e sonar opteyn & getyn pi desyr, & now it is grantyd *p*e. I wyl no lengar *p*ow fast, *p*erfore I byd *p*e in *p*e name of Ihesu ete & drank as thyn husbond doth. (chap 11)

With eating, drinking and praying under a cross by the roadside they celebrated their treaty. So her fight for her own body was won. She had achieved a first in recorded history.

To my knowledge this is the earliest extant English document of a woman fighting and winning the battle for her own body. But, at the same time, this is yet another passage that testifies to the duality in Margery Kempe's life. When she dedicated herself to Jesus, this did not undo her marriage vow for life; she did not break her earthly promise and, apart from the time she spent travelling, stayed with her husband, caring for him in his old days.

She managed to create and retain her privacy, and Jesus kept her aware of her luck:

> Dowtyr, 3if *p*u wilt bethynk *p*e wel, *p*u hast rith gret cawse to lofe me abouyn al thyng for *p*e gret 3yftys *p*at I haue 3yftys *p*at I haue 3ouyn *p*e be-for-tyme. & 3et *p*u hast an-o*p*er gret cawse to louyn me, for *p*u

75

hast þi wil of chastite as þu wer a wedow, thyn husbond leuyng in good hele. (chap 65)

We know she was conscious of a related sense of duality, for, when she was accused of being a Lollard and imprisoned in Leicester, she begged:

> I prey ȝow, ser, put me not a-mong men, þat I may kepyn my chastite & my bond of wedlak to myn husbond, as I am bowndyn to do. (chap 46)

The culminating evidence for the spiritual balance she achieved can be seen in her description of nursing her husband, senile and incontinent as he was, as though he were Christ Himself.

> þan sche toke hom hir husbond to hir & kept hym ȝerys aftyr as long as he leuyd & had ful mech labowr wyth hym, for in hys last days he turnyd childisch a-ȝen & lakkyd reson þat he cowd not don hys owyn esement to gon to a sege, er ellys he wolde not, but as a childe voydyd his natural digestyon in hys lynyn clothys þer he sat be þe fyre er at þe tabil, weþyr it wer, he wolde not sparyn no place. And þerfor was hir labowr meche þe mor in waschyng & wryngyng & hir costage in fyryng & lettyd hir ful meche fro hir contemplacyon þat

> many tymys sche xuld an yrkyd hir labowr saf sche bethowt hir how sche in hir 30ng age had ful many delectabyl thowtys, fleschly lustys, & inordinat louys to hys persone. & perfor sche was glad to be ponischyd wyth þe same persone & toke it mech mor essily & seruyd hym & helpyd hym, as hir thowt, as sche wolde a don Crist hym-self.
> (chap 76)

For years she had been trying to atone for her failings. Finally, she appears to have achieved a sense of being at one with her ambitions. In its original sense, she found "at-onement": at least in retrospect, she seems to have been able to assimilate her worldly past into her aims, thus coming to terms with the duality inherent in her life.[1] She was given the chance to accept the mundane part of her life although it clashed with her later heavenly aspirations. She was able "to reinterpret and reincorprate her sexual past into her spiritual vocation, a process revealed in her return to care for her sick husband, when she defines anew her lifetime of physical involvement with him".[2]

When she was about forty and had probably just come into some money after her father's death, she felt the desire to see more and visit the places of Jesus' birth and passion. She got Jesus' full support. He told her that He would always protect her and be with her wherever she went. In 1413, having paid her debts, she travelled alone to the Holy Land.

Jesus commanded her to wear white as a sign of her chastity. Although she was afraid that she, a married woman,

---

[1] Random House Dictionary: to at-one: backformation from atonement: archaic: reconciliation, agreement, from phrase at + ME onement

[2] Angela Lucas, *Women in the Middle Ages. Religion, Marriage and Letters* (Brighton Sussex; Harvester, 1983) p xxiii.

would be attacked for wearing the colour of virginity, she agreed. Her fears materialized and, in fact, she was interrogated on the subject frequently. At Cawood, for instance, she was questioned by the Archbishop: "Why gost *þu* in white? Art *þu* a mayden?" (chap 52). The fight for her white clothes actually continued until finally, probably around 1414, Jesus commanded her to see her "hir gostly fadyr, Wenslawe be name" and tell him to give her permission to wear white as that was the Lord's wish, "& so weryd sche white clothys euyr aftyr" (chap 37).

Possibly this demonstration of a battle won suited her basic need for the public display that we know from other passages in the *Book*. In the course of her quest for approval, Jesus advised her to meet with many doctors of divinity, bishops and other religious persons; Julian of Norwich was one of them and their conversation is recorded in some detail in chapter 18 of the *Book*.

Margery Kempe discussed her revelations with these experts. Some believed her and others doubted her genuineness. As evidence of supernatural powers she was able both to reveal secrets (chap 12) and to predict events: "Sche knew & vndyrstod many secret & preuy thyngys whech schuld befallen aftyrward be inspiracyon of *þe* Holy Gost" (proem, chaps 25, 71, and 89). This second sight seems to have impressed many of her antagonists, lay as well as ecclesiastical, men as well as women.

Often she was accused of being a Lollard, of having the devil within her. She was imprisoned and threatened with burning at the stake but, with Jesus at her side, she cleverly negotiated her way out. Cautious, yet determined, she must have been very convincing as she was able to disarm many strong opponents. She knew her Bible and quoted it wisely. Thus she cited Luke xi, 27/28 when defending her right to speak of her experiences and of the Lord. Once again, when accused of being a Lollard and when commanded by the Archbishop in York to swear not to preach to the people in his diocese, she retaliated:

> Nay, syr, I xal not sweryn, for I xal spekyn of God and vndirnemyn hem þat sweryn gret othys wher-so-euyr I go vn-to þe tyme þat þe Pope and Holy Chirche hath ordende þat no man schal be so hardy to spekyn of God, for God al-myghty forbedith not, ser, þat we xal speke of hym. And also þe Gospel makys mencyon þat, whan þe woman had herd owr Lord prechyd, sche cam be-forn hym wyth a lowde & seyd 'Blyssed be þe wombe þat þe bar & þe tetys þat ʒaf þe sowkyn.' þan owr Lord seyd a-ʒen to hir, 'Forsoþe so ar þei blissed þat heryn þe word of God and kepyn it.' And þerfor, sir, me thynkyth þat þe Gospel ʒeueth me leue to spekyn of God. (chap 52)

In another of these interrogations some people, hoping to prove that she was a heretic, asked her whether she was of Christian or Hebraic faith.[1]

Travelling in these times was hazardous. Margery was repeatedly ill, possibly with dysentery: "Sche had þe flyx a long tyme tyl sche was anoynted, wenyng to a be deed" (chap 56). It is interesting to see that the sacrament of extreme unction which may have caused, at least to some extent, Julian of Norwich's decision to become an anchoress and to withdraw from the world, is only used by Margery Kempe to illustrate the seriousness of her condition and seems to have had no further significance for her spiritual progress.

---

[1] As there were no Jews living in England at that time the word "Jew" was probably used for unbelievers in a rather general, derogatory sense. This can be substantiated by an article of Regula Heusser's who has observed that in twentieth century Japan, where there is no Jewish population, antisemitic tendencies are particularly strong. "Forschung zur Fremdenfeindlichkeit in Europa," *Neue Zürcher Zeitung* 260 7./8. November 1992: p25.

79

Some other mysterious infection troubled her with extreme pains

> during þe terme of viij 3er, saf viij wokys, be diuers tymes. Sumtyme sche had it onys a weke contunyng sumtyme xxx owrys, sumtyme xx, sumtyme x, sumtyme viij, sumtyme iiij, & sumtyme ij, so hard & so scharp þat sche must voydyn þat was in hir stomak as bittyr as it had ben galle, neþyr etyng ne drynkyng whil þe sekenes enduryd but euyr gronyng tyl it was
> gon. (chap 56)

Her travelling-companions were understandably extremely annoyed with her at times and treated her cruelly.

> They cuttyd hir gown so schort þat it cam but lytil be-nethyn hir kne & dedyn hir don on a whyte canwas in maner of a sekkyn gelle, for sche xuld ben holdyn a fool & þe pepyl xuld not makyn of hir ne han hir reputacyon. (chap 26)

Her fits of weeping, the need to demonstrate her special status with the Lord, and, last but not least, her position as a married woman trying to live the life of a saint disconcerted men as well as women:

> & þerfor many man & many woman wondyrd up-on hir, skornyd hir & despised hir, bannyd hir & cursyd hir, seyde meche euyl of hir, slawnderyd hir, & born hyr on hande þat sche xuld a seyd thyng whech þat sche seyd neuyr. (chap 45)

She was repeatedly left behind in countries whose language she did not speak and had to find new travelling-companions. On numerous occasions she was insulted or had her belongings stolen, but there were always kind people to help her and she found it in herself to forgive her tormentors. Her discussions with Jesus, who always assured her of His love and the worthiness of what she was doing, gave her strength to persist.

> Dowtyr, þis plesith me rith wel, for þe mor schame & mor despite þat þu hast for my lofe, þe mor joy schalt þu haue wyth me in Heuyn, and it is rithful þat it be so. (chap 78)

She bore all unpleasantness gladly, remembering the agonies Jesus had suffered for mankind and joyfully identifying with him in her pain. However, she was often very much afraid. During one of the many interrogations she had to endure she was left standing alone while her tormentors went to find fetters to chain her.

> Than sche mad hir prayers to our Lord God al-mythy for to helpyn hir & socowryn hir ageyn alle hir enemys, gostly and bodily, a long while, & hir flesch tremelyd & whakyd wondirly þat sche was fayn to puttyn hir handys vndyr hir cloþis þat it schulde not ben aspyd. (chap 52)

She focused in her narrative on the many incidents that happened as she travelled; seemingly petty events are often rendered in great detail. Her itineraries are only mentioned in passing, but one instance may be worth noting. Some time after having crossed the Channel, they came to a place called "Seryce" (chap 26), just one day's travel from Constance. Conceivably she visited Zurich to pay homage to Felix and Regula, or Zurzach to pray to Verena. Zurzach was called "Zurciacum" around that time and was an important trading center for woollen cloth and cloth dying materials among other things. Because of the important wool trade there I tend to believe that it was Zurzach she visited. On the other hand, both towns belonged to the bishopric of Constance and therefore "Seryce" could stand for either of the two names.[1] Given the rudimentary attention her travels get, and taking into consideratio n that she dictated the *Book* so many years later, she may have been confused about the order and spelling of the towns which she passed through. She was aware of this problem:

> Yf þe namys of þe placys be not ryth wretyn, late no man meruelyn, for sche stodyid more a-bowte contemplacyon þan þe namys of þe placys, & he þat wrot hem had neuyr seyn hem, & þerfor haue hym excusyd. (*BMK* II, chap 4)

By way of Assisi, she continued to Rome where she visited the chapel of St. Bridget, the Swedish Saint whose cult in England at that time was considerable and who was probably known to Margery Kempe. She prayed in the Church of the Apostles, where her mystical union with the Lord took place.

She finally arrived in Jerusalem, entering the city riding on an ass. On Mount Calvary she had a vision of Christ on the Cross and her weeping reached a new level. Whenever she was reminded in the remotest sense of Jesus her shrieking became louder, and she often lost consciousness.

---

[1] For more information see *"Historisch-Biographisches Lexicon der Schweiz"*. Band 7, Neuenburg: 1934.

Fyrst whan sche had hir cryingys at Ierusalem, sche had hem oftyn-tymes, & in Rome also. &, whan sche come hom in-to Inglonde, fyrst at hir comyng hom it comyn but seldom as it wer onys a moneth, sythen onys in *p*e weke, aftyrward cotidianly, & onys sche had xiiij on o day, & an-o*p*er day sche had vij, & so as God wolde vistiten hir, sumtyme in *p*e cherch, sumtym in *p*e strete, sumtym in *p*e chawmbre, sumtyme in *p*e felde whan God wold sendyn hem, for sche knew neuyr tyme ne owyr whan *p*ei xulde come. & *p*ei come neuyr wyth-ow tyn passyng gret swetnesse of deuocyon & hey contemplacyon. (chap 28)

Her seizures must have been frightening:

> ...sche fel down *p*at sche myght not stondyn ne knelyn but walwyd & wrestyd wyth hir body, spredyng hir armys a-brode, & cryed wyth a lowde voys as pow hir hert xulde a brostyn a-sundyr, for in *p*e cite of hir sowle sche saw veryly and freschly how owyr Lord was crucifyed. (chap 28)

These loud fits persisted for ten years and some of them lasted five or six hours. But she also wept more conventionally for her own sins and for the sins of others, as described in chap 57.

Because of these attacks she was often not admitted to hear mass or receive communion with others. Eventually the Lord delivered her from her loud crying, so that she could go to church again without disturbing anybody. Yet there were others who approved of her gift and envied it. People asked her to pray for them and some wanted her to be present at their deaths. So in some vague way she became something similar to a death counsellor, and a professional lamenter.

In 1415 she returned to England but kept travelling locally until in 1417 she set out for Santiago.

> & so *þ*ei abedyn *þ*er xiiij days in *þ*at lond, & *þ*er had sche gret cher, bothyn bodily & gostly, hy deuocyon, & many grett cryes in *þ*e mende of owr Lordys Passion, wyth plentyuows terys of compassyon. (chap 45)

It was at this time that her vivid imagination enabled her to feel present at the scene of the Passion.

Her search for recognition went on during the years when she nursed her sick husband, lost both him and her son, and travelled to Danzig in order to accompany her daughter-in-law back home. She prayed for others in need, for souls in purgatory, and preached the goodness of the Lord whenever she got the opportunity. Preaching became an obsession with her and she must have enjoyed the drama that often went with it. When she was yet again arrested for heresy, threatened with the stake and shut up in a house, she opened the window and preached to the people in the street.

> *þ*an stode sche lokyn owt at *þ*e wyndown, tellyng many good talys to hem *þ*at wolde heryn hir, in so meche *þ*at women wept sor & seyde wyth gret heuynes of her hertys, 'Alas, woman, why xalt *þ*u be brent?' Than sche preyd *þ*e good wyfe of *þ*e hows to ȝeuyn hir drynke, for sche was euyl for thryste. And *þ*e good wyfe seyde hir husbond had born a-wey *þ*e key, wherfor sche myth not comyn to hir ne ȝeuyn hir drynke. And *þ*an *þ*e women tokyn a leddyr & set

> up to þe wyndown & ȝouyn hir a pynte of wyn in a potte & toke hir a pece, besechyng hir to settyn a-wey þe potte preuly & þe pece þat whan þe good man come he myth not aspye it. (chap 53)

Though this incident can be explained by her uncontrollable need to be noticed, it certainly required remarkable courage to do as she did. Furthermore, this passage illustrates that where there were women who despised her, there were also those who sympathized with her, ran some risk by hearing her preach, and were willing to help her.

Through listening to holy men speak she was able to intensify her meditating:

> So be processe of tyme hir mende & hir thowt was so ioynyd to God þat sche neuyr forȝate hym but contynualy had mende of hym & behelde hym in alle creaturys. (chap 72)

The more she believed in her revelations, the more Jesus rewarded her with His presence. She received particular thanks from Christ for specific endeavours such as her compassion towards Him and others, her fight against swearing, breaking the commandments, living in sin, and for enduring for His sake.

She, unlike Julian of Norwich, was informed by the Lord of the time of her own death (chap 74).

(iv) Experience Mirrored in Margery Kempe's *Book*

The metaphors and similes employed by Margery Kempe are generally powerful and easily understood, partly because, due to her lack of any formal training, she drew on her background as a housewife. Jesus assured her of their mutual love by saying she adhered to Him "as *þ*e skyn of *þ*e stokfysche cleuyth to a mannys hand whan it is sothyn" (chap 37). The man who had propositioned her told her later that "he had leuar ben hewyn as smal as flesch to *þ*e pott" (chap 4) than sleep with her. On the other hand, alliteration and other stylistic elements, such as word pairs, seem to have been used instinctively.

Her descriptions are especially vivid where she relived her own experiences, as in the description of a woman who went mad after a difficult childbirth, undoubtedly a representation of her own crisis:

> ...sche knowyth not me ne non of hir neyborwys. Sche roryth & cryith so *þ*at sche makith folk euyl a-feerd. Sche wyl bo*þ*e smytyn & bityn, & *þ*erfor is sche manykyld on hir wristys. (chap 75)

This in part recalls the account of her own illness in chapter 1:

> And also sche roof hir skyn on her body aȝen hir hert wyth hir nayles spetowsly, for sche had non o*þ*er instrumentys, & wer sche wold a don saf sche was bowndyn & kept with strength bo*þ*e day & nyght *þ*at sche myght not haue hir wylle.

The brilliance and captivating immediacy of the scene cannot be simply have been envisioned, but must have been endured in all its mediaeval gruesome intensity by the writer herself.[1]

When she, swaddling Jesus, told him:" Lord, I schal fare fayr with ȝow; I schal not byndyn ȝow soor. I pray ȝow beth not dysplesyd wyth me" (chap 6) one could suspect that she, who seemed to testify to only the smallest interest in her own children, at least for a while did experience maternal, protective instincts. But then, once she (like other mothers) had buried each child she needed to shield herself from grief at the loss. The infant mortality rate was very high: "...the woman laboured under the handicap of constantly bearing children - most of whom soon died and had to be replaced" (Trevelyan, p 61). Actually, her description of herself caring for Mary as a child and her participating actively at the birth of Jesus add another facet to the fragmentary picture of Margery Kempe as a mother found elsewhere in the *Book*.

The immediacy of her involvement is important for an analysis of Margery Kempe's personality; in her visions she seems to have been compensating for many of her real-life deprivations. She was conceivably counterpoising the death of most of her own children by visualizing herself present at the birth of a baby who, we all know, did survive. She mentioned giving birth fourteen times in chapter 48 but only talked about one son. Possibly the trauma of losing one child after another left her emotionally starved and she may have settled for substitutes. This theory finds substantiation in chapter 35. She was ready to see the child Jesus in every baby:

[1] The unbelievable suffering of women in childbirth has been documented in, for example, the much later *"The Autobiography of Mrs. Alice Thornton ,"* (1627-1707) ed. C. Jackson (Surtees Society 62, 1875)

Sche was so meche affectyd to þe manhode of Crist þat whan sche sey women in Rome beryn children in her armys, 3yf sche myth wetyn þat þei wer ony men children, sche schuld þan cryin, roryn, & wepyn as þei sche had seyn Crist in hys childhode. And, yf sche myth an had hir wille, oftyn-tymes sche wolde a takyn þe childeryn owt of þe moderys armys & a kyssyd hem in stede of Criste.

So complete an identification could have brought release from her own loss and grief. Modern psychology stresses the importance of an "idea" to cling to for the digestion of traumata.

An indication that she may finally have been able to overcome the injuries suffered through the loss of her own children is found in chapter 1 of *Book* II. She mentioned her own granddaughter in a rather touching way, calling her "a fayre mayde-child", which is a more tender description than that allowed to anyone human elsewhere in Margery Kempe's *Book*.

More remarkable is her description of the mystical marriage to the Lord in Rome:

> And þan þe Fadyr toke hir be þe hand in hir sowle be-for þe Sone & þe Holy Gost & þe Modyr of Ihesu and alle þe xij apostelys & Seynt Kateryn & Seynt Margarete & many oþer seyntys & holy virgynes wyth gret multitude of awngelys, seying to hir sowle, 'I take þe, Margery, for my weddyd wyfe, for feyrar, for fowlear, for richar, for powerar, so þat þu be buxom & bonyr to do what I byd þe do. For, dowtyr, þer was neuyr childe so buxom to þe modyr as I xal be to þe boþe in wel & in wo, - to help þe and comfort þe.' ... And þan þe Modyr of God & alle þe

seyntys þat wer per present in hir sowle preyde þat þei myth haue mech joy to-gedyr. (chap 35)

Later, Jesus told her:

> I take non hed what þu hast be but what þu woldist be. And oftyn-tymes haue I telde þe þat I haue clene for3oue þe alle thy synnes. þerfore most I nedys be homly wyth þe & lyn in þi bed wyth þe. Dowtyr, thow desyrest gretly to se me, & þu mayst boldly, whan þu art in þi bed, take me to þe as for þi weddyd huisbond, as thy derworthy derlyng, & as for thy swete sone, for I wyl be louyd as a sone schuld be louyd wyth þe modyr & wyl þat þu loue me dowtyr, as a good wife owyth to loue hir husbonde. & perfor þu mayst boldly take me in þe armys of þi sowle & kyssen my mowth, myn hed, & my fete as swetly as thow wylt. (chap 36)

As she spoke of having heard about other women mystics, she may have known the account of Mechthild von Magdeburg's mystical marriage, a representation of remarkable intensity, which possibly influenced or encouraged her. Margery Kempe's description of the mystical union does not specify whether she was married to God, the Father, or God, the Son. Both spoke to her during the ceremony. Traditionally, a mystic's union was with the Father, yet she was particularly drawn to the Son as she had seen him in her first vision - a beautiful young man.

The author of the *Book* is repeatedly reproached by unsympathetic critics such as Louise Collis (p 146) or Susan Dickman (Margery Kempe and the Continental Tradition of the Pious Woman, p 161) for losing spiritual reference when she connected divine experience with impressions of everyday life.

They accuse her specifically of mixing crude realism with transcendental matter in her attempt to describe the ineffable. This criticism could easily be answered by pointing to similar juxtapositions in the "Song of Solomon". Particularly unfair are the accusations that Margery Kempe left the spiritual level when she compared the song of a redbreast to heavenly music in chapter 36. Few have found fault with the beautiful compositions to birds' voices by Händel and later by Mozart and Wagner. Nobody has even thought of criticizing any of these composers for exaggerated earthiness when choosing such themes. This brings us back to the problem mentioned earlier of categorizing texts according to literary genres. Because the *Book* has been catalogued with divine texts, passages mingling the heavenly and the mundane invite sharp criticism. Wrong expectations lead to disappointment.

If we are treating Margery Kempe as more than an eccentric, we need to measure her against her own principles. Strictly sincere, she behaved in accordance with her religious and social convictions, preferring to adapt to rather than violate tradition. What is important is the way she recounted and digested her constant communication with the Divine. By relating her achievement to the writings of other women we can gauge her importance.

(v) Why She Wrote

I have arrived at a point now where the motivation for Margery Kempe's writing at all ought to be evaluated.

She found one clear reason for writing in God's command to make a book of "hir felyngys & hir reuelacyons" (proem). Since we are considering wish-fulfillment as a constant possibility, however, we must assume that His command was a projection of her desire to put her feelings into words.

This assumption is justified by the numerous instances where Margery Kempe's subconscious appears to have suggested patterns of behaviour that in one way or another were acceptable or even desirable to her. Her extrovert character would certainly account for 'going public'.

But there are other considerations. I have suggested that she could have been suffering from some guilt. The sin that sent her into the bout of madness after the birth of her first child is often alluded to in the *Book* but never put into words. Could she be appealing to the reader to absolve her? Is the *Book* a vindication, then? Since she had no audience in the form of grandchildren, another possible motivation would be her realization that unless she created some record, unless she changed from oral to written testimony, her undoubtedly unusual life would eventually be doomed to oblivion. Dictating and at the same time reliving her experiences obviously gave her much pleasure:

> Also, whil *þe* forseyd creatur was occupijd a-bowte *þe* writyng of *þ*is tretys, sche had many holy teerys & wepingys, & oftyn-tymys *þ*er cam a flawme of fyer a-bowte hir brest ful hoot & delectabyl. (chap 89)

Although a White Friar had suggested much earlier that she write down her experiences, she waited for God's command. Actually, as early as 1413, when Margery Kempe and her husband visited Bishop Repingdon in order to make their vows of chastity, he had advised her to write down her experiences "seying þei wer hy maters & ful devout maters & ensyred of þe Holy Gost, cownseling hir sadly þat hir felyngys schuld be wretyn." (chap 15) As "þe sayd creatur had continued hir lyfe þorw þe preseruyng of owr Sauyowr Crist Ihesu more þan xxv ʒer whan þis tretys was wretyn" (chap 87), it must have been around 1420 that she began dictating her *Book* to the first scribe,

> a man dwellyng in Dewchlonde whech was an Englyschman in hys byrth & sythen weddyd in Dewchland & had þer boþe a wyf & a chyld, hauyng good knowlach of þis creatur & of hir desyr, meued I trost thorw þe Holy Gost, cam in-to Yngland wyth hys wyfe & hys goodys & dwellyd wythþe forseyd creatur tyl he had wretyn as mech as sche wold tellyn for þe tym þat þei wer to-gydder. (proem)

The Lord assured her that her writing pleased Him although she did not have as much time for her prayers as she had had before:

> Drede þe not, dowtyr, for as many bedys as þu woldist seyin I accepte hem as þow þu seydist hem, & þi stody þat þu stodiist for to do writyn þe grace þat I haue schewyd to þe plesith me ryght meche &

92

he þat writith boþe. For, þow 3e wer in chirche & wept bothyn to-gedyr as sore as euyr þu dedist, 3et xulde 3e not plesyn me mor þan 3e don wyth 3owr writyng, for dowtyr, be þis boke many a man xal be turnyd to me & beleuyn þerin. (chap 88)

The amanuensis, who may or may not have been her son, died before the *Book* was completed. Some information on this can be found in the proem and chapters 15 and 89.

The fruit of their efforts was an almost indecipherable text which was "neiþyr good Englysch ne Dewch, ne þe lettyr was not schapyn ne formyd as oþer letters had ben" (proem).
Only after great effort did she persuade a priest to begin rewriting it. In 1436 the last ten chapters of *Book* II were added. Apart from a record of some of Margery Kempe's prayers, *Book* II is to some extent a report of her son's life and death and her subsequent trip, accompanying her daughter-in-law back to Danzig.

It is rather intriguing to see that while in *Book* I, she made little mention of her offspring, *Book* II deals to a large degree with her son and his family. I very tentatively suggest the possibility that, through having been able to accept all stages of her life and integrate them, through "at-onement" in the original sense, Margery Kempe was finally able to talk about her son, the fruit of her "fleschly lustys", which for so long had been a problem to her. Detached as she had become, she experienced the greatest Grace: the awareness of independent responsibility.

V MARGERY KEMPE'S STANDING

a) Julian of Norwich and Margery Kempe -
Contemporaries Compared

"Julian of Norwich and Margery Kempe of Lynne break a long tradition of feminine silence in England; though as women as unlike as two human beings could be, as writers and mystics they may to some degree reflect similar foreign influences" (Allen, p llxii).

The only two acknowledged representatives of women writers of fifteenth century England present us with apparently contrasting pieces of literature. How far apart they were in their personalities is difficult to say; we know literally nothing about one and a plenitude of self-confessed detail from the other.

Extrovert, outgoing in every respect, Margery Kempe is really quite easily understood by a sympathetic reader. Introvert, withdrawing, even secretive, Julian of Norwich hid in every possible way and no amount of empathy will give a student of the *Revelations* more than a conjectural impression of the author's personality. The author allowed her reader no distraction from her main goal: to find out about the wonderful love of God.

The perseverance, almost stubbornness, with which Margery Kempe pursued her endeavours is in strong contrast with the complying submission, for which Julian of Norwich has earned approval. Where Margery Kempe chose a dual life, Julian of Norwich lived the one-track life of an anchoress.

In theory, however, either's writing results from the same aspiration: the mystical development of the authoress. Their need made them fall back on what their culture had to offer. They interpreted their mission according to their characters. Where Julian regressed to a womb-like, enclosed state, Margery Kempe freed herself from the bounds of tradition and became in the vitalistic sense an entity.[1]

The purpose of the following section is to point out differences and find similarities which, in the end, should also enable us to detect any affinities in either book to what has recently been termed the women's liberation movement.

I shall try to define whether the situation of either woman anticipated the move towards independence still in progress in the twentieth century.

Both women stood out from the norm. Yet for one writing was the only deviation, in all other aspects she conformed. By withdrawing according to the accepted pattern of a mystic; by constantly protesting her allegiance to the Holy Church; by shaping her writings according to proven literary patterns of male mystics, she found approval from all circles and at all times. There are no indications of any attack against her person or thinking to be found anywhere in the *Revelations*.

On the other hand Margery Kempe's unorthodox behaviour must have taxed to the breaking-point the patience and tolerance of both the clergy and lay people she met. Despite hostility from some priests, she was tolerated by the church. Hope Emily Allen has suggested that one of the reasons for her acceptance might have been the clergy's awareness of contemporary mysticism on the continent:

---

[1] "The primary difference between Vitalism and the classic philosophic schools is this. Its focal point is not Being but Becoming." (Underhill p 28)

At the same time, it seems to me that whatever were the causes that made Margery Kempe what she was, the theory of foreign influence helps to explain why her obviously cultivated and conscientious confessors allowed her to continue in a type of mysticism which at many points would almost certainly have been condemned by the Middle English mystical writers whom we know to have been read in their world. The learned clerical supporters of Margery may have been, to some degree at least, swayed in their judgement of her by knowledge of the distinguished support given abroad to feminine writers who, however admirable in some ways, also gave precedent for emotional and egoistic demonstrations like hers (*BMK*, Prefatory Note, lv)

Both were carried in their actions by an immense feeling of love: Julian of Norwich's urge to teach stemmed from a wish to share her private happiness with her beloved brethren; Margery Kempe's chosen life-style made manifest her personal love for the Divine.

In Margery Kempe's case her extravagant claims led to ostentatious behaviour, which provoked much disapproval. Julian of Norwich, though at times highly emotional, has never been accused of shrill absurdity; she spared her environment the embarrassment of physical demonstrations. The only reason for which she could have been reproved, the fact that she was a woman, she suppressed. She was virtually untouchable.

As pointed out in an earlier chapter, Julian of Norwich loved her brethren so deeply that she wanted them to partake in her sublime experience. Her love for God and her deep feeling for His children made her write. It is interesting to see that the far more independent Margery Kempe waited for God's command before she started writing. A possible awareness of the additional

97

problems that could arise from breaking yet another unwritten law may have been the cause for her refusing Bishop Repingdon's suggestion to write down her experiences. In the proem she described how people had offered to record her feelings and revelations but "sche was comawndyd in hir sowle þat sche schuld not wrytyn so soone" and "so it was xx ȝer & mor fro þat tym þis creatur had fyrst felyngys & reuelacyons er þat sche dede any wryten". The Lord wished her to publish her life with the many proofs of His goodness and love for her. We must not forget that on more than one occasion Margery Kempe seems to have tailored the divine commands, at least to some extent, to accommodate the needs of the heavenly way on earth. The celestial orders she received would not interfere with her daily chores. There is the further consideration that the Lord's command to make her unusual life public was a projection of her personal wish to make known to others what she had achieved.

To differentiate between the two, one could consider their various interpretations of the word "love". The calm Julian of Norwich pondered her insights and came to bland, orthodox conclusions which she presented in immaculate shape. Boisterous Margery Kempe, through intuition rather than cognitive process, sensed the implications of love and idiosyncratically did what she felt needed doing in order to make known God's compassion.

We are in possession of two documents treating the same subject. Both texts describe unions with divine figures. However, apart from the actual visions which differed in both their nature and their frequency, the contrasting personalities of the two writers made the *Revelations* and the *Book* into two very different treatises. In the case of Margery Kempe it became a personal narrative about a warm partnership. The *Revelations*, on the other hand, are a generally controlled report of divine love with occasional outbursts of emotions. The discrepancy between the two authoresses is further defined when we remember that the recording of experiences seems to have been Margery Kempe's preoccupation, whereas Julian of Norwich's didactic intention caused her to match style to content: what Cicero termed 'decorum'.

Julian of Norwich's communion was spiritual. She gazed at her vision of the passion and received teachings during the span of one night; Margery Kempe, the housewife, had continual dalliance with manifestations of either God the Father or God the Son and her partnership was almost tangible.

Margery Kempe's glowing report of the "wonderful spechys & dalyawns whech our Lord spak and dalyed to hyr sowle" (proem) strongly constrasts Julian of Norwich's analytical delineation of how "Alle thys blessyd techyng of oure lorde god was shewde by thre partys" (chap 73: 2-3).

The anchoress seems to have spent her days totally occupied in explaining her divine revelations. Margery Kempe, however, as mother, housewife, miller, brewer, had "iiij owrys of þe for-noon in holy speeches & dalyawns wyth owr Lord" (chap 59). However disparate the circumstances, both writers seem to have experienced immense joy and pleasure in their visions.

The goal of both women was to understand the love of God. Their characters, however, led to diverging interpretations. Where one felt she needed to withdraw and concentrate exlusively on her personal studies, the other metabolized divine advice and put it into practice. Instead of retreat, she chose travel. Like Penelope's, Julian of Norwich's voyages were of the mind. Prayer and meditations in her cell were sufficient for her. Though to Margery Kempe too they were of critical importance, she needed more. So sensuous was she that she had physically to travel, tread the paths, to identify with her Lord's immediate background. By describing herself entering Jerusalem riding on a donkey, she allowed her readers a glimpse of this involvement.

As I pointed out in the respective chapters, both Julian of Norwich and Margery Kempe had to deal with the big problem common to all mystic writers - they were trying to communicate something basically ineffable. Therefore we must look at their writings keeping in mind Wittgenstein's words: "Das Unaussprechliche ist - unaussprechlich - in dem Ausgesprochenen enthalten." This procedure may enable us to find out what lies hidden within the texts.

A short recapitulation of the preceding chapters shows that Julian of Norwich, on the one hand, subordinated herself almost completely to the demands made on women by the clergy and a male dominated society. By writing in the vernacular she was merely in keeping with the trend at that time. Brant Pelphrey sees the work of Julian of Norwich as one of the most representative examples for Middle English Prose.[1] He stresses that before her no woman had written in this language, that the vernacular became the official language at about the same time, and that mystic theology reached its peak in that era. (Assuming that she really did not know Latin, she of course could have written in no other language.) Allowing that writing in the vernacular was her one innovation, her methodical approach to expressing the inexpressible testifies to high intelligence and exceptional resilience.

---

[1] Brant Pelphrey, *Love Was His Meaning: The Theology and Mysticism of Julian of Norwich*, Salzburg Studies in English Literature under the Direction of Professor Erwin A. Stürzl. Elizabethan and Renaissance Studies 92:4, Editor: Dr. James Hogg. Institut für Anglistik und Amerikanistik, (Salzburg:Universität Salzburg, 1982)

Margery Kempe, on the other hand, is the creator of a very different document. Written in restrospect and dictated to at least two unknown scribes, it takes the form of an autobiography - the first in the English language - and is the testimony of an impressive search for identity. Why it was written in the third person singular has provoked numerous suggestions. Marlena Corcoran has proposed that the very title *The Book of Margery Kempe* signifies proprietary indication. "The book is both by and about her and the title may also suggest that it belongs to her" (p 4). However, this particular grammatical usage was also common with continental mystics. A true mystic considers himself to be the mouthpiece of the divine, a medium for the message. Conceivably, Margery Kempe was able to step back and review her life from a distance, which may have encouraged her to use this specific grammatical form.

Whatever the reasons, the *Book* is a document of tremendous value to the researcher into the history of women's quest for identity and independence.

By violating no demands made on women by the church, Julian of Norwich was eligible for its support and, if necessary, protection. However, as I have noted in the sections on the style and content of the *Revelations*, her intelligence enabled her to deal in an independent way with impressions received either directly through her visions or from other mystics' texts. Although Margery Kempe gave the appearance of being more dependent, seeking advice and protection from any number of people, she proved her independence when her behaviour blatantly contravened tradition. By going the heavenly way while still performing most earthly duties, she pragmatically questioned the values imposed on women.

For Julian of Norwich the revelations and their interpretation was a means to an end; for Margery Kempe the inspirations resulted in her life taking a different form. The *Random House Dictionary* defines meditation as "thought, reflection, contemplation, a thinking over". Both women did indeed digest their divine inspirations. Where with Julian of Norwich the act of meditation became an end in itself and the kernel of her teachings, Margery Kempe went one step further and, instead of withdrawing, put her personal understanding of God's love into practice, amalgamating meditation and action.

Margery Kempe experienced Jesus as a beautiful young man and interpreted the visions according to her previous earthly experience. Her God was there just for her, interested in her as a person, sympathizing with her and trying to help with even the smallest worries. She found in the Godhead practical advice as well as a partner who talked to her, who always had time for her and made no physical demands; in short her Deity represented everything that she must, consciously or subconsciously, have found lacking in her life.

Julian of Norwich encountered a maternal, yet more distant God who told her not to pry, assured her that all would be well and that He was in command. She experienced Deity according to the mystic tradition as a loving omnipresence. On this important point Margery Kempe and Julian of Norwich agreed. Both found in religion and the accompanying visions something that they did not find in real life. Where the anchoress probably projected her deep, frustrated needs and found fulfillment in the figure of God as mother, Margery Kempe found a partner that would have been her dream-man in earthly life. These explanations do not contradict the existence of a deep religiosity in the two women. On the contrary, it was their practiced, experienced religion that provided relief from worldly problems and release of pent-up frustrations.

To the anchoress Trinity required analysis and she presented it attractively; the wife of John Kempe saw Holy Trinity as part of the ecclesiastical repertoire, an accepted factor not requiring any special attention.

At one time or another both women experienced doubts about the veracity of their divine inspirations but neither hesitated when it came to executing the orders they conveyed.

Food as nourishment for the body finds no mention in the *Revelations*. I have drawn attention to the fact that Margery had enjoyed the physical side of life before she turned to the heavenly way. In chapter 5, when Jesus ordered her to stop eating meat, he did so with the following words: "*þ*u must forsake *þ*at *þ*ow louyst best in *þ*is world & *þ*at is etyng of flesch". Orders to fast or to give up fasting resulted in an effect strongly resembling today's so-called eating disorders. She may have suffered from yet another syndrome common to twentieth century women, that of being "out of order" due to the pressure to conform. It was not only in sexual matters that Margery Kempe sought control of her own body. If eating disorders manifest internal stress, her stop/start diet possibly illustrates the conflict inherent in her duality. By trying to reconcile the demands of the mundane and spiritual worlds, she was moving towards defining a room of her own.

Margery Kempe was a very feminine and provocatively female being. She was aware of her sex and sexuality and consequently feared for her chastity. In the *Book* we find overt and hidden indications of what must have been a healthy sexual drive, which she wanted to suppress. In my opinion, the divine orders for chastity were undoubtedly a result of her own understandable wish for the cessation of continual pregnancies, the dangers of childbirth, and, as was seen especially in her case, the often ensuing loss of the child. Her negotiating what in German is called a "Josefs-Ehe", a chaste marriage, really a contradiction in terms, is another illustration of the duality of Margery Kempe's aspirations. She was forced to deal with problems outside the cloistered one-track existence of Julian of Norwich.

As pointed out above, Julian of Norwich's vision of Satan may have been indicative of a suppressed sexuality, yet there is no perceptible evidence of it in either her writings or in what we know of her life.

Where Julian of Norwich was able to integrate sin in the divine concept of salvation and accept its necessity, Margery Kempe greatly feared and fought sin in herself and in others by preaching against it and suffering for the sins committed by herself and others.

Both women were willing to suffer. Her prayer for suffering was a dominant factor in the mystical development of Julian of Norwich. Margery Kempe gladly suffered all the tribulations the heavenly way involved but never asked for them.

Extreme unction, as we have seen, was merely a way of illustrating the seriousness of her illness with Margery Kempe. Julian of Norwich on the other hand experienced it as a trigger mechanism in her mystical development

Where Margery Kempe greatly feared death, Julian of Norwich longed for it. Paradoxically, the Lord did not inform the anchoress of the time of her death. Yet Margery Kempe received exact information about her span of life.

I started out this passage of my considerations with the fact that the authors of the texts in our hands left the norm. They, both women, broke new ground by daring to write. Furthermore, they made public personal experiences, a subject not previously considered worth any attention. Julian of Norwich is the better stylist and meets more of the required characteristics of a mystic. True mystic that she was, her message - a work of art - was on a transcendental level. Practical Margery Kempe, however, the illiterate "would-be-saint" with her much-questioned qualities, produced a work that has bearing on women's issues today.

Traditionally Julian of Norwich has been considered superior to Margery Kempe both as writer and theological commentator. By contrasting their treatment of selected points I hope to have indicated that although faultless Julian of Norwich has drawn great applause, Margery Kempe made the greater contribution to feminist awareness: where Julian could accept her status as a woman because to her everything was part of the whole creation, Margery Kempe, the doer, fought to circumscribe her own sphere. Julian of Norwich was not concerned with change. Margery Kempe did challenge male dominance.

For these reasons Margery Kempe functions as the kingpin in my attempt to trace early stages of the liberation of women.

b)   Margery Kempe - A Milestone

I have so far been dealing with the two best-known early representatives of writing women in England. I began my survey with Julian of Norwich, whose *Revelations of Divine Love* is both in style and in contents typical of the mystical writing of the time.

By approaching Margery Kempe through a consideration of both Julian of Norwich's work and pertinent criticism, the amazing difference between the two near-contemporaries has been accentuated. Julian of Norwich, the archetype of the mediaeval feminine mystic, fitted literary as well as sociological patterns and has found approval from her own times to the twentieth century. Influenced by the general tenor of commentators dealing with both Julian of Norwich and Margery Kempe, I expected on the one hand to find the daughter of John Brunham a hysterical, unbalanced woman, unjustifiably driven to record the story of her life. I thought that her work would reflect similar dealings with divine instructions and reactions to spiritual contacts as Julian of Norwich's as well as a corresponding lifestyle. Such assumptions invite biased criticism and have gnerally caused the *Book*, to be deemed inferior to the *Revelations*.

Moreover, the *Book* remained almost totally unknown: no references have been recorded apart from the two excerpts mentioned above (pp 53-54).

After its re-emergence from five hundred years of obscurity, *The Book of Margery Kempe*, although innovative, was regarded as a mystical text, a definitely minore one at that, and scholars have ignored its other messages. Only today have researchers such as Wendy Harding begun to see the timelessness of Margery Kempe's implied claims.[1]

By assessing her through her own account rather than in the shadow of Julian of Norwich, and by reflecting on some overlooked aspects of her life, I have been able to gauge the importance of Margery Kempe's insights. I came to the conclusion that she foreshadowed the emergence of a sense of their own importance in women. Although there was no perceptible link to any successors, what she did, in fact, was to anticipate what could be called the women's movement of the early eighteenth century.

Douglas Gray included Margery Kempe and her *Book* in a survey of popular religious enthusiasts and, rather than blame it for not being on the level of Julian of Norwich's *Revelations*, saw it as a remarkable expression of the vitality of fifteenth-century religion.[2] Though less dismissive than many, Gray seems to have overlooked its contribution to social history. However, his approach might indicate that scholarly opinion is ready for a reappraisal of Margery Kempe's standing. If we see her as a forerunner of a phenomenon that only took shape much later, then she is the prototype of a perennial model - a human being, denied its rights and fighting for them.

As I have frequently claimed, there are certain prerequisites without which any desire for creativity cannot be fulfilled. We have seen that one of these necessitites is a private sphere.

---

[1] Wendy Harding, "Body into Text, *The Book of Margery Kempe,*" *Feminist Approaches to the Body in Medieval Literature*, eds. Linda Lomperis and Sarah Stanbury (Philadelphia, University of Philadelphia Pess, 1993) pp 168-187.

[2] Douglas Gray, "Popular Religion and Late Medieval English Literature," *Religion in the Poetry and Drama of the Late Middle Ages in England,* eds. Boitani, Piero, and Anna Torti (Cambridge: D.S. Brewer, 1990)pp 1-28.

The *Book* - created in the enclave of her relation with the divine - is our key to the author. Other women may have taken to writing, perhaps reacting to frustration, but no other mediaeval manuscripts, evidence of literary creativity, have been discovered. Creativity, as evinced by childbirth, family care, and religious duties, leave no record that we can analyse. Literature, especially accounts like the *Book*, can provide the scholar with more than just a factual account. Margery Kempe has set out for us her reaction to unhappiness and her resultant joy. Inevitably, individuals may react to deprivation in a negative way, too. Examining the consequences of destructive response to frustration, while interesting, is not relevant to a study focussing on literary creativity.

Taking Margery Kempe as an example, I plan to investigate writings of the following two hundred and fifty years, hoping to determine the nature of various women's reactions to pressure and any ensuing creativities. That is, I hope to document the latent desire for individuality and different paths proposed towards a possible achievement of that goal.

When I studied Julian of Norwich and Margery Kempe, looking for common aspects, I found frustrations or deprivations that, together with a strong need for wish fulfillment, could have set in motion their acts of liberation.

In the case of Julian of Norwich we have no evidence for the causes of her withdrawal. Yet I have sketched a possible interpretation of her idea of God as mother. If we accept projection as a viable possibility, frustrated need for maternal warmth may have caused her to visualize the ideal mother. Her creation was so immensely convincing to her that she began to record it for the benefit of her fellow Christians.

With Margery Kempe matters are somewhat easier to identify. Her *Book* gives such a wealth of intimate information that we can correlate her desire for chastity with her need for a room of her own. Thanks to this unusual woman we have a record of tendencies towards a liberation of women existing in the early fifteenth century, and thus long before any women's movement was defined, this extrovert individual produced a testimonial of extraordinary importance to the student of the history of women.

At first sight, the *Book* seems no more than a life-story dictated by the rather unbalanced protagonist, who many years earlier had gone mad, probably due to post-partum depression, and later chose the heavenly way after her miraculous recovery. In her Prefatory Note to *The Book of Margery Kempe,* Hope Emily Allen points out that signs of mystical awakening and growth are clearly discernible (*Book,* Prefatory Note, pp liii-lxviii). Yet her subsequent religious efforts, in which vision, reality, imagination, and wishful thinking coalesced, resulted in her becoming a would-be mystic at best. She was therefore considered no more than a rather unimportant contemporary of the well-known Julian of Norwich, the respected recluse and author of the *Revelations of Divine Love*, whose prophetic assurance that all will be well has rung out over the centuries.

After the first excitement of the discovery of the Butler-Bowden manuscript in 1934 there was a sense of let-down. As I have pointed out (above p 51) in the interval between Margery Kempe's dictating the *Book* and the publication of fragments in 1521 the fallacious idea that she was a recluse had grown and her text has been attributed to the "ancres Margery Kempe". As she was neither anchoress nor woman of letters, the application of

109

traditional criticism to the *Book* as a mystical text proved inappropriate.

Her experiences were deemed too earthy to testify to true mystical exposure and her style has been judged crude. Wolfgang Riehle actually cites her as an example for the decline of the mystical movement:

> On the other hand, Margery Kempe, who lived in the first half of that century, documents by her particular mysticism how at the same time the decline of the movement was prepared.[1]

Yet only two years after the publication of Riehle's paper, Douglas Gray, as already mentioned, showed a more positive approach.

Although the overall influence of the scribes on the text is not finally determinable, in my opinion, a basic genuineness can be attributed to the *Book* for at least this reason: a man could be expected to have endowed Margery Kempe with what were considered feminine virtues, such as submissiveness and constraint, rather than the masculine independence she displayed.

The *Book*, which is the earliest known autobiography in English, has an attractive spontaneity of style and diction. Moreover, it is an exceptional historical document of the life of a somewhat strange woman of the fifteenth century.

Setting aside, therefore, any considerations of its religious or literary distinction, I was free to approach her *Book* from a woman's point of view. In this light her achievements have a far greater importance than that so far attributed to Margery Kempe,

---

[1] Wolfgang Riehle, "Research and the Medieval English Mystics" *Genre, Themes, and Images in English Literature.* eds. Boitani, Piero, and Anna Torti. (Tübingen: Gunter Narr, 1988) p 142.

the housewife of Lynn. She is an ideal kingpin because the conditions of her life reflect the situation of women in general, and her accomplishment relates to aspects that have universal bearing on the plight of women. We may safely assume that feelings of frustration at her failures and actual deprivations such as the deaths of most of her children caused her to withdraw into a world of her own choosing. She exemplifies Virginia Woolf's theory that a room of one's own is a prerequisite for creativity:

> But, you may say, we asked you to speak about women and fiction - what has that got to do with a room of one's own? I will try to explain. ... All I could do was to offer you an opinion on one minor point - a woman must have money and a room of her own if she is to write fiction; (*A Room of One's Own*, p 6.)

Whether Margery Kempe's work be considered autobiography or fiction - the requirements for either writing are clearly the same.

It was against all odds that the *Book* was written. The question why it was written invites a multitude of answers. In general women at that time were not aware of their own importance, and the need to leave records of their personal lives for further generations did not manifest itself for another century and more. Admittedly, Margery Kempe was a theatrical woman; as we have seen, she liked to stand in the limelight. Being the main character in a book, furthermore a book she had authored, would appeal to her. However, more important was her implicit sense that her achievements had so far justified her efforts and her idea that her trials and tribulations needed to be preserved for posterity. Having lost her only surviving child, she may have felt that "Unlook'd on diest, unless thou get a son".[1] She may have decided to provide an offspring in the form of her *Book*.

Thanks to her deviation from the contemporary norms in lifestyle and in writing we have this early evidence of an incipient wish for more freedom. Her *Book* heralds the timeless case history of a woman seeking fulfillment outside the prescribed sphere.

Margery Kempe wanted out. Her wish to travel was only a physical expression of an inner desire. Without severing them completely, she found a way of loosening the social ties in her life. If we assume that the subconscious controls to some extent our dreams and visions, it was her magnificent buoyancy at the time of intense insanity that produced salvation in the form of the initial vision. As Sonja Rüttner-Cova, a psychoananlyst, has pointed out, Margery Kempe's overall behaviour suggests the presence of a very strong "kundalini", the eastern mystical concept of a force for survival (in private discussion, December 1990). Honed by a post-partum depression almost certainly combining with exhaustion and frustration, her innate will to live forced her to create an escape. Just as some of the world's greatest scientific innovations have occurred despite - or because of - inauspicious conditions, so it was extremity that made Margery Kempe produce the life-saving revelation.

Fortuitous for the history of feminism, the cloak of holiness allowed her to move into a niche sanctioned by contemporary society. While following the heavenly way, she saw opportunities available to a woman in her situation and made instinctive use of them.

In keeping with her extraordinary character, she did not shake off her responsibilities. She stuck with what she had

---

[1] William Shakespeare, Sonnet vii, l 14.

promised. A certain restlessness felt throughout the *Book* could possibly have been caused by the tension between her inner and her outer world - by the clash between her wishes and reality. The conflict between what she wanted to do and what the demands of the situation around her allowed her to do could have produced this impression of constant searching. With the one exception that she chose to refuse the sexual obligations in her marriage, she fulfilled the earthly duties of a married woman as far as her pilgrimages permitted.

Her wish for chastity, more than a means to ending her pregnancies, can be seen as a demonstration of liberation. In some Swiss German dialects the word "Gmächt" (room) is used for vagina in a human.[1] The word "Schloss" in the sense of "lock" has the meaning of vulva in a dog. Margery Kempe's custodianship then can be interpreted as the concretion of a more general achievement: by denying her husband access to her body, she symbolically claimed the right to a room of her own.

How unusual she was can be seen in the admirable strength with which she coped with the strain of this duality. The deep certitude that what she did was absolutely right carried her through all the difficulties and finally permitted her "at-onement" to which the *Book* is proof.

Moreover, her writing proves that, once won, the private sphere enabled her to develop into a human being according to her own definition. Furthermore, it evoked a creativity that would otherwise have lain dormant. Thus Margery Kempe's work is evidence for the suggestion that a "room of one's own" ultimately permits creativity.

---

[1] Titus Tobler, *Appenzellischer Sprachschatz* (Zürich: von Orelli, Füssli & Compagnie,1837)

Throughout, the *Book* remains a testimonial of devotion. However, Margery Kempe's line of thought is accessible even to the religiously unconditioned mind. Unspoilt by education, the author did not feel a need to follow any literary pattern. Describing her visions in her eccentric way, she set down a detailed anamnesis of the becoming of a person. Her descriptions of the divine inspirations presumably mirror the way she actually experienced them. The *Book* is a tangible definition of the personality of its author.

Another most important aspect of the text is that it is the first record of the concept of rape in marriage. I have pointed out in a preceding chaper how deeply concerned Margery Kempe was with this issue. In addition to the dread of the actual violation, I can see a more generalized fear of being trespassed on, of being denied a chance of self-rule. While I have been working on this project, Swiss law has been changed to concede that intercourse, even in marriage, must be an act of volition, not obligation.[1] The issue is still under debate in Great Britain and not even discussed in many other countries, but in the early fifteenth century, Margery Kempe successfully defined a private sphere by opting for a chaste life.

The way she dealt with her marriage vows shows a determined yet concerned trait. Even when she refused her husband his rightful access to her body, she remained his wife. I have repeatedly pointed out indications of the dualism inherent in the life of Margery Kempe. However, her nature enabled her, if not at the time, at least in retrospect, to come fully to terms with the dichotomy of her chosen life. Ernest Schachtel, a

---

[1] Schweizerisches Strafgesetzbuch, Militärstrafgesetz, Art. 190,2 was enacted to become effective as of October 1, 1992.

psychoanalyst, discusses this ability in relation to childhood memories:

> Memory as a function of the living personality can be understood only as a capacity for the organisation and reconstruction of past experiences and impressions in the service of present needs, fears and interests ... Just as there is no such thing as impersonal experience, there is also no impersonal memory.[1]

Her book is the extreme demonstration of Margery Kempe's potential to find solutions which may seem fluid yet which never clouded her integrity. Written when she was an old woman, her selective recollections have reconciled conflicting elements. Celibate yet married, a mother yet childless, tradesman yet mystic, aware of the flesh yet committed to her heavenly way, illiterate yet an authoress, she nevertheless appears to her readers as an indivisible individual. That this dualism in the life of an apparently unbalanced creature never led to schizophrenia is clear indication of her psychological resilience.

Bridging the apparent schism by focusing on one aspiration and so finding an inner equilibrium, she was able to reconcile, to "at-one", all aspects of her existence and thus find fulfillment through leading a life in praise of God according to the directions she was given by Jesus in her visions. The interpretation of these divine instructions according to her earthy nature led to a practical approach towards her goal. She needed no more special gifts than her instinctive expertise as a housewife, businesswoman, and mother.

---

[1] Ernest Schachtel, *Metamorphosis* (1959; New York: Da Capo, 1984) p 128.

Her gateway to heaven was homely and therefore was open to even the most simple and uneducated mind. Where Rolle specifically addressed the recluse, Hilton the intellectuals and Julian of Norwich the mystically inclined, Margery Kempe wrote for everyman. Her method is demonstrated in practice, therefore more accessible than any beautifully worded theories.

Moreover, she did have one rare asset: she was able to pursue her endeavours without basically neglecting any existing promises. She did what she felt she needed to do without making others pay for her personal satisfaction.

Although she provoked anger by not fitting any pattern, she apparently never hurt anybody when following through what she saw as divine instruction. Indeed, throughout her life she remained accountable.

Despite the hard-won independence from her husband, it was with a male that she formed her ideal relationship. The extent to which she was conditioned by her environment can be illustrated by this fact. Having won the struggle for her own spiritual "room", she subordinated herself to yet another male controlling figure; the figure of Jesus In Margery Kempe's life was as real as any earthly man. The continuous, intimate support of this surrogate partner is a captivating aspect of the story.

However great her achievement was, it is obvious that she was exceptionally lucky with regard to her immediate personal situation. She was leaving her husband in more ways than one. Although he was willing to please her, I doubt that he would simply have let her set off on her pilgrimages had there been children to look after. I question his willingness to tolerate her coping with civil indictments had they interfered with the running of a large household. However, he may have been realistic enough to see the positive side of their agreement of chastity. His permitting her to live a physically independent life may to some extent have suited his needs. I tentatively suggest the possibility that he too, feeling grief at the loss of one child after another, condoned her independence.

In addition, her abrasive behaviour could have irritated him so much that he would even appreciate her going off on her own at times. In that case such a solution may conceivably have suited their mutual need for separate rooms of their own.

> Women have served all these centuries as looking-glasses possessing the magic and delicious power of reflecting the figure of man at twice its natural size. (*A Room of One's Own*, p 35)

Two hundred years later, the Duchess of Newcastle conventionally portrayed her husband, politically inept though he must have been, in a heroic light. Margery Kempe - yet again ahead of her times - was confident enough to present an unexpurgated picture of her marginalized husband. This realistic attitude seemed to enable her to acknowledge his share in her "Becoming", a term I have used when discussing her spiritual development.

As to her caring for him in his days of sickness, we know the reasons for her commitment. It was the simple transcription of her marriage vows to stay with him "in sickness and in health". Also, in keeping with her interpretation of divine love, it was her practice to help her fellow-humans in need. Perhaps though, she was subconsciouly aware of the almost schizophrenic situation that although she did not want any physical love from him, without her husband, she would have had no pregnancies, no births, no post partum depression and therefore no visions. She may thus even have felt some sort of gratitude, an individual experience of "felix culpa", when she realized that, after all, he was instrumental to her progress.

Whatever the circumstances behind her story, qualities such as those exemplified by Margery Kempe enable a woman at any time in history to find a life of her own.

She did not fit any set pattern of her time and therefore her contemporaries could not do her justice. On the other hand it is this unconventionality that makes working with the author of the *Book* so very fascinating: where her own contemporary values were not applicable, twentieth century customs offer any number of possibilities for comparison.

She was a forerunner of a movement that was not to begin until centuries after her death. Therefore present day scholars are better equipped to evaluate and appreciate her achievements than were her contemporaries. The way she dealt with her situation and fought for her ideas is as effective now as it was then. Her problems are as relevant to present day women as they were to her.

VI A ROOM OF ONE'S OWN

All living beings have to endure some suffering, what Buddhists call "samsara". However, how much can be endured before a reaction sets in is a matter of the individual character. The thresholds of tolerance vary from person to person and greatly depend on the respective genetic and environmental background. Why some women suffered and others thrived under the same conditions is a question of temperament: a question of the plant either bending with the wind or snapping. Generally we can say that happiness is an indicator of an ability to accept. Inevitably, then, it is the unhappy human beings that are the innovators. Or, as the historian, Max Silberschmidt put it in one of his lectures: "Full bellies do not start revolutions." However, finding universally applicable rules for defining the point at which a reaction occurs is virtually impossible.

Acknowledging indefinable parameters in both individual characters and situations, it is as futile to try to define the causes of a reaction as to predict the course the liberation will take. Throughout history there must have been as many ways of relieving pressure as there were women who sought escape, and the shape each private sphere was given depended on character and circumstance.

Let us consider specifically women's potential for freedom in a man's world at the end of the Middle Ages. "The Wagoner's Lad", descended from oral tradition, neatly sums up the situation:

> Controll'd by their parents
> Until they are wives.
> Slaves to their husbands
> The rest of their lives.[1]

Woman's role was very closely defined and she was trained into submission by society and church. No free choice was offered. Instruction was restricted to household and breeding matters. Girls, regarded as chattle, were more of a burden than an asset and they were married off as soon as possible and at as low a dowry as possible. Female offspring deemed unfit for marriage were, if genteel, frequently sent to a convent or, when less fortunate, ended up as domestics in wealthier houses.

No encouragement for seeking privacy was given. Education was generally available to girls only as second hand information. A possible source for erudition in wealthy homes would be eavesdropping on brothers' lessons, or surreptitious study of the boys' homework. The reading material eventually consumed was mainly religious. Frequently, feelings of guilt prevented the pursuit of studies begun in secret, and therefore many clandestine attempts at self-expression were destroyed. Education for women was tolerated only when it benefitted men. Furthermore, the church proclaimed suffering a virtue. In sermons, the subjection of women was reinforced. By blocking off possibilities for literacy, the danger of influences through new ideas was kept at a minimum.

---

[1] Although eminent folk-singers like Joan Baez and Peggy Seeger have recorded this South Appalachians folk-song, neither has succeeded in tracing its origin. Almost certainly it has been handed down by generations of women singers and was carried across the Atlantic. A similar version has been recorded in England by the Watersons who acknowledge no written source either The subtle variations of each live performance.testify to the vigour of an oral tradition which has not been frozen by formal editing.

Education was considered akin to sinfulness and the root of all evil in the female sex. Once married, a woman was fenced in with domestic duties. Any ideas about becoming an individual merely hovered in the background, sometimes finding expression in a diary, and often dying a silent death. The conditions for producing a piece of art were indeed dire. Virginia Woolf's statement can be applied to the Middle Ages as well as to our times:

> But for women, I thought, ... these difficulties were infinitely more formidable. In the first place, to have a room of her own, let alone a quiet room or a sound-proof room, was out of the question. (*A Room of One's Own*, p 51)

However, there were exceptional women who, in spite of adverse conditions, did cross the barrier. From being defined by men, they made their way to a sphere where they could decide for themselves and become individuals. Unfortunately, few early texts by women are available and we must use those we can lay our hands on. Margery Kempe's *Book* and Julian of Norwich's *Revelations* are such pieces of writing. However, they are so different from each other that it seems hard to believe no other women of that period produced any texts within that range. Therefore, we must assume that a number of texts were lost; some may still lie hidden, waiting to be discovered and shed new light on the prerequisites for creativity.

By definition, there are innumerable kinds of creativity. Writing is but one, yet verbal communication has advantages over non-verbal creative acts such as painting or embroidery. It is more easily interpreted. In addition, feelings preserved in "these black lines"[1] and protected in libraries had a better chance of survival .

Some of these creative results manage to live and others, by nature, do not. Recipes or remedies, for example, were absorbed into tradition, where track of individual authorship was lost.

By studying numerous prose texts written by women before 1700, I was able to detect one common aspect: the authors of all the works in one way or another had been conscious of suffering. It is my aim to substantiate the idea that this suffering may liberate the energy to construct some bubble of private territory. This "room" initially consists of a vacuum that beckons to be filled, an area inviting exploration. I have come to the conclusion that a personal realm must be something very close to Virginia Woolf's "room". "A Room of One's Own" can therefore be considered if not a *sine qua non* then at least highly conducive to creativity.

My intense preoccupation with the *Book* and my ensuing empathy for its author led me to see a quite different picture of this mediaeval woman than has hitherto been presented, as I have been trying to show.

---

[1] William Shakespeare. Sonnet lxiii, l 13.

Using the specific example of Margery Kempe I want to explore this more general idea that the awareness of frustrations[1] or deprivations[2] sets free one's strength to gain room, to fight for a private territory and homerule. I hope to show how in this acquired space, personality can develop to make individual creativity possible.

The importance of both character and background for this development has been demonstrated by the examples of Julian of Norwich and Margery Kempe. The opposites of bending to convention on the one hand and challenging tradition on the other enabled these women to testify in writing to their achievements.

---

[1] Oxford Advanced Learner's Dictionary: to frustrate: prevent (sb) from doing sth

[2] Oxford Advanced Learner's Dictionary: to deprive: take away from; prevent from using or enjoying

VII SEARCH FOR SUCCESSORS TO MARGERY KEMPE

a)   The Fate of the *Book*

The analysis of the two authors so far considered has already contributed support to the notion that "a room of one's own" is a necessity for creativity. Julian of Norwich's withdrawal into an actual cell and Margery Kempe's choice of chastity as a symbolized private sphere equally substantiate this assumption.

Tangential to my initial research, I became increasingly aware of another point of interest related to the idea of a private sphere, equally important as a prerequisite for creativity for men and women, yet of an essentially feminist significance. Twentieth century commentators, such as Bridget Hill[1], have defined the feminist movement as a phenomenon that began to take recognizable shape three hundred years ago. Was not *The Book of Margery Kempe* a much earlier manifestation of a woman's successful bid for liberation?

From what appeared merely the autobiography of a unbalanced woman of the fifteenth century, evidence for the existence of feminist claims emerged - the very claims still preoccupying women today. Encouraged by these findings to believe I had found the root of a development, I expected to trace a continuation of this process.

However, my aspirations were disappointed. Although from the fifteenth century on the rising bourgeoisie became conscious of the importance of education and literacy was more widespread among women, no known document of the next

---

[1] Bridget Hill, ed. and intro. *The First English Feminist. Reflections Upon Marriage and Other Writings by Mary Astell* (Aldershot: Gower, 1986)

centuries written by a woman shows signs of dissatisfaction with the lot of its authoress. Only very few biographies and no autobiographies of women seem to have been written in the sixteenth century.

That simply no texts of this kind were written and Margery Kempe's document was in fact unique must at least be taken into consideration. But let us assume that more autobiographies were written and due to adverse circumstances were lost. That all texts were lost seems highly unlikely. What happened to the *Book* could have happened to other works and the odd one would have reappeared.

The Book of Margery Kempe had a chequered fate. The subsequent publication of selected passages distorted its actual message; it was ascribed to an anchoress. When, after five centuries, it became accessible again, a vague assumption that it was a mediaeval mystical text subsequently caused disappointment among critics as well as uncertainty as to its genre. All of these circumstances eventually resulted in its dubious fame as a literary embarrassment, a curiosity at best.

Though it showed its protagonist aspiring to a religious life, the first autobiography in English was unable to satisfy its readers' expectations of a spiritual record, and therefore it was ignored or used only as a foil to accentuate the high standard of the contemporary *Divine Revelations*. Therefore, later scholars were liable to approach Margery Kempe with preconceptions that blinded them to her real importance.

Although my own first approach to Margery Kempe was inevitably coloured by existing interpretations, I was fortunate to be able to use the complete version rediscovered in the middle of this century. I realized her *Book* had been inadequately categorized and came to view it as the testament of a woman, of a practical, devout wife. To my mind *The Book of Margery Kempe* emerged as a work of even greater significance than is suggested by its usual epithet: the first autobiography in English.

By printing only parts selected for their religious interest, Wynkyn de Worde inadvertently omitted any passages now seen to be of feminist value. It would be anachronistic to imply that his choice was due to hostility: feminism had not then been defined. Yet it is in those sections of Margery Kempe's work which he dismissed that we now find a first determined articulation of feminist awareness in England.

b)   Women Writing (15th to 17th Centuries)
After having realized the enormous importance of Margery Kempe's document, I made a close study of the prose writings, religious and secular, by women in the years between her death and the year 1700. I was hoping to find further evidence of what was later to be termed feminism.

I was greatly helped by *Early English Books 1475-1640* and *Early English Books from 1641-1700*, however taxing the prolonged use of microfilm may be. For much secondary material and for texts written before but published after 1700, and subsequently not included in the UMI collection, I had to rely on libraries in Europe and the U.S.A. Nevertheless, I have read the available prose writings by women in England before 1700, and studied pertinent critical reactions.

In substance I agree with the findings and opinions of recent editors. Scholars such as Hilda Smith, Mary Prior, Moira Ferguson, Katherine Usher Henderson and Barbara F. MacManus, and Elaine Hobby have produced excellent studies that can be used as a basis for any research in this field. In addition, compilations such as "The Norton Anthology of

Literature by Women", Janet Todd's two dictionaries, and the recent bibliography concerning female writers before 1800, by Hilda Smith and Susan Cardinale, are excellent aids to the study of literature of that period by women in English.[1]

Despite a meticulous search for either a parallel to Margery Kempe's achievement, or a development of what she had begun, concrete evidence failed to emerge. Careful analysis of texts that were written in the three centuries after Margery Kempe's death allowed only occasional glimpses of an underlying unhappiness with women's lot. Although isolated writers were of particular interest, far from showing the independence the author of the *Book* had demonstrated most women seemed resigned to accepting the traditional dominance of the male.

Letter writing by women has never provoked pejorative comment. In consequence, collected letters have a spontaneity which makes them authentic documents of women's lives and feelings. Irrespective of the content, and whether expressing joyful or sad feelings, such texts generally resulted from separation, perhaps from deprivation caused by the absence of a friend or relative. Women's letters from that period, though they covered a range of subjects, generally manifest a passive acceptance, rather than indignation at their lot. One exception is the seventy seven letters of Dorothy Osborne who frankly set down for her intended husband, William Temple, her ideas of a partnership in marriage.[2] Clearly, this real-life woman felt misgivings about male dominance. Apart from stressing the importance of a similar background of the couple, she stipulated

---

[1] Full titles see my bibliography

[2] Edward Abbot Parry, ed., *Letters from Dorothy Osborne to William Temple 1652-1654* (London: S.M.Dent, 1914)

a trial marriage for one year before a definite commitment was made. However, her prudent negotiations were confined to a private exchange of letters.

Royal correspondence dealing with matters of state was collected by Mary Ann Everett Green-Wood, although we have no idea of the editorial principles - other than availability - by which she made her selection.[1] Anthologies of letters such as those by Margaret Paston (1440-1484)[2] and her less known relative, Katharine (1578-1628)[3], as well as throwing light on contemporary domestic affairs, charm the reader with the immediacy of a mother's concerns and a wife's longing for her absent husband. In contrast, the letters of Rachel Wriothesley, Lady Russell (1636-1723), written in the years after the death of her husband, depicted the course of mourning.[4] This record of her feelings could provide a case history for theories as propounded by modern psychologists.[5] Anne Finch Viscountess

---

[1] Mary Ann Everett Wood-Green, Letters of Royal Ladies of Great Britain from the 11th Century to the Close of Queen Mary's Reign(1846)

[2] Norman Davies, ed., *Paston Letters and Papers of the Sixteenth Century* (Oxford: Clarendon, 1971)

James Gairdner, *The Paston Letters* 1422-1509 (London: Constable, 1900)

[3] Ruth Hughey, *The Correspondence of Lady Katharine Paston 1603-27* (Norfolk Record Society vol 14, 1941)

[4] Lord John Russell, ed., *The Letters of Rachel Wriothesley, Lady Russell.* From the manuscript at Woburn Abbey with an introduction vindicating the character of Lord Russell against Sir John Dalrymple etc. and the trial of William Russell for High Treason (London: J. Dove, 1826)

The Letters of Rachel Lady Russell (London: Longman, 1853)

[5] J. Bowlby, *Verlust und Trauer* (Frankfurt: Fischer, 1983)

Thomas Charlier, "Ueber die pathologische Trauer," *Zeitschrift für Psychoanalyse und ihre Anwendungen* 10, Jahrgang 41, Oktober 1987.

Conway, author of the philosophical treatises "Opuscula Philosophica" and "The principles of the ancient and modern philosophy", both published after her death, corresponded with Henry More over a period of several years.[1]

In 1664, Margaret Cavendish, the eccentric Duchess of Newcastle, who experimented with most contemporary literary genres, took a first step in the direction of the epistolary novel and prepared the way for authoresses such as Aphra Behn, whose *Love letters Between a Nobleman and His Sister* (1684-1687) sold widely. The Duchess of Newcastle adapted the sanctioned literary form of letter-writing for voicing her opinions in her *CCXI Sociable Letters*. In short epistles to "a friend" she reacted to accusations against her person, discussed general topics such as the effect of age on women's beauty, commented on incidents in society and outlined her ideas on a welfare system.

Keeping a diary is nowadays a "widely acknowledged tool of psychotherapy" because "in the act of writing a sequence of transformations may occur as unconscious matter presents itself to consciousness for assimilation".[2] While it seems justified to see a growing sense of self-importance underlying women's need to record their lives and experiences for posterity, the therapeutic effect of re-living the day vicariously is undeniable. The genre of diary-writing developed over the next centuries. As Harriet Blodgett points out in her anthology of English diaries by women, *Capacious Hold-All*: "There is no one diary style" (p 2). However, journals progressed from the meticulous documentation of religious self-examination, prayers and

---

[1] Margery Hope Nicolson, ed., *The Correspondence of Anne, Viscountess Conway, Henry More and Their Friends 1642-1684* (New Haven: Yale University Press, 1930)

[2] Harriet Blodgett, *Centuries of Female Days, Women's Private Diaries* (New Brunswick: Rutgers University Press, 1988) p 3.

meditations to the documentation of personal ideas. Where the earliest known diary by Lady Margaret Hoby, begun in 1599, is a detailed book-keeping of religious duties performed, towards the end of the seventeenth century, Lady Lettice, Viscountess Falkland, expressed in her journal hopes for better educational possibilities for women.[1] Although suggesting "places for the education of young gentlewomen, and for retirement of widows ... hoping thereby that learning and religion might flourish more in their own sex than theretofore", she seems to have taken no action. However, her predecessor, the Duchess of Newcastle, had actually addressed writings to distinguished universities, calling for higher education for women in the preface to her *Philosophical and Physical Opinions*: "To the Two Most Famous Universities in England" (1655). In addition she had written "The Female Academy"(1662), "a drama centring on women's intellectual development in a separatist environment".[2] If marginally more active, in terms of battling the male bastion of learning, the Duchess of Newcastle's appeal was little more than the raising of a suppliant hand. Like Lucy Hutchinson (1620-?), translator of the six books of Lucretius into English, who attached an autobiographical fragment to her eulogy of her husband, the Duchess of Newcastle added her own "True Relation of My Birth, Breeding and Life" to her husband's biography, *The Life of ... William Cavendishe*. Anne Clifford, Countess of Pembroke, Dorset and Montgomery (1590-1676) prefaced her diary with a short autobiography. While these appendices could be interpreted as signs of independence, Mary

---

[1] M.F. Howard, ed. and intro., *Lady Lettice Vi-Countess Falkland* (London: John Murray, 1908) p 28.

[2] Kate Lilley, "Blazing Worlds: Seventeenth Century Women's Utopian Writing," *Women, Texts and Histories*, eds. Clare Brant and Diane Purkiss. Brant, (London: Routledge, 1992) p 107.

Beth Rose, in "Gender, Genre and History", considers the Duchess of Newcastle's "True Relation" an "illustrative failure insofar as she begins with and ends the work by defining herself through others" (p 299).

During the fifteenth century the rising bourgeoisie became conscious of the importance of education (see above, p 55). Translations such as Margaret Roper More's English rendition of Erasmus' "A Devout treatise on the Paternoster" in 1525 indicate that literacy was spreading among women. Margaret Tyler's English version of the first part of *The Mirrour of princely Deedes and Knyghthood* by Diego Ortuñez de Calahorra appeared in 1578. The "Epistle to the Reader" seems important as it justifies her role as the translator of a chivalric tale in a time when women's writings were traditionally confined to religious texts. Undoubtedly, these translations testify to their originators' erudition, yet they cannot be interpreted as expressions of their authors' dissatisfaction with the lot of women.

The reign of Elizabeth I might have been conducive to a rising sense of independence among women. However, the high esteem for the virgin queen seems to have been mainly a personal idolization and led to no claim by her women contemporaries for general change. One possible exception must not be overlooked because, to all appearances,

> *Jane Anger her protection for women. To defend them against the Scandalous Reports of a Late Surfeiting Lover and all other like Venerians that complain to be overcloyed with women's kindness* (1589)

could be mistaken for an active demonstration of a surfacing feeling of equality. The author of this first published female contribution in England to the debate about the superiority of men over women "argues her case with fierce partisanship and considerable wit, often turning her 'protection' of women into an indictment of men" (Henderson/McManus, p 14). The identity of the writer is unknown and it seems likely that the name "Anger" was chosen to represent a frame of mind. Helen Andrews Kahin and other researchers have been unable to agree on a contemporary written provocation for this sharply polemic text.[1] Whether Jane Anger's indignation is to be termed personal or general, it indicates that in the Elizabethan era there was some awareness of a controversy about the "querelle des femmes", originated in 1399 by Christine de Pizan with her *The Book of the City of Women*. Yet though with Elizabeth I's accession to the throne one of the most spectacular eras in English history began, when she "managed to stimulate an esprit and self-confidence in her subjects unmatched in English history"[2], the spirit she instilled in her people as a whole had no lasting effect on the self-esteem of her female subjects.

In the first half of the following century, publications like Constantia Munda's *The Worming of a mad dogge: or, a soppe for Cerberus the Jailor of Hell. No Confrontation but a Sharp Redargutation of the Bayter of Women* (1617), Rachel Speght's *A Mouzell for Melastomus, the cynical bayter of Evahs sex.* (1621), and Mary Tattlewell's and Joan Hit-Him-Home's *The womens sharpe revenge: or an answer to Sir Seldome Sober.* (1640) reacted to attacks from men who felt threatened by articulate women. These authoresses responded to such provocation as Joseph Swetnam's *The Arraignment of Lewd, Idle, Froward and Unconstant Women* (1615) by retaliating in kind, and therefore

---

[1] Helen Andrews Kahin, "Jane Anger and John Lyly," *PMLA* 8 (1947): pp 31-35.

[2] Harold J. Schultz, *History of England* (New York: Barnes & Noble, 1980) p 97.

their output lacked originality. Although they were aware of the symptoms of their serious predicament, because they failed to address its cause, their efforts were doomed to fail. Moreover, as Diane Purkiss points out, these texts were in fact published pseudonymously and the gendering of the authors remains open to discussion.[1]

A continuous feature underlying many texts is both the fear of confinements and child mortality. In the Book of Common Prayer, a special service, the Churching of Women, enabled a family or a community to give thanks for a safe delivery, which implies that the deaths of both mother and child were common occurrences. In her will, dated 1610, Lady Anne Newdigate expressed her wish "that my boys be brought up in good learning and both they and my daughter to be brought up in virtuous and godly life."[2] Margaret Godolphin (1672-1696) mapped out plans for the life of her unborn child in case of her own death in childbed. In diaries and letters women often described their terror of imminent confinement or grief at yet another child's death. Elizabeth Joceline's "The Mothers legacie to her unborne child", published in 1624, movingly reflects an expectant mother's dread of impending suffering. Surprisingly, none of the writers advocated Margery Kempe's radical solution.

In the period of the Civil Wars, women had to perform many duties of their absent men, some of them venturing into the field of religious statement and controversy. "More and more women refused to stay silent in the great religio-political questions of the day, and took to prophesying in churches,

---

[1] Diane Purkiss, "Material Girls: The Seventeenth Century Woman Debate," *Women, Texts and Histories 1575-1760*, eds. Clare Brant and Diane Purkiss (London: Routledge, 1992)

[2] Antonia Fraser, *The Weaker Vessel* (London: Weidenfeld & Nicholson, 1984) p 121.

marketplaces and in the street. Some of them wrote down and published their messages" (Hobby, *Virtue* p 27)· Between 1643 and 1652 Eleanor Douglas wrote profusely about her premonitions and predictions but seems to have been an embarrassment rather than a serious contributor to the intellectual reputation of women. In 1687 another prolific writer, Elinor James, published her most famous essay,
"Mrs James's vindication of the Church of England, in an answer to a pamphlet entitled, "A new Test of the Church of England's Loyalty", where she defended the Declaration of Toleration of James II. Like her other twenty nine tracts, it was published by herself and signed with her full name.

A large number of broadsides and petitions written, or at least submitted and signed, by women imply a growing political awareness. In 1649, Joanne Cartwright petitioned for the readmission of Jews into England.[1] The Leveler, Katherine Chidley, in 1653, presented a petition signed by six thousand women protesting to Parliament against the affluent lifestyle of its members. Printed advertisements for businesses run and products manufactured by women appeared. Women reacted in print against unjust accusations. Midwives began to defend their position in medicine against men. Jane Sharp's handbook in six volumes *The Midwives Book or the whole art of Midwifery discovered. Directing childbearing women how to behave themselves. In their conception, breeding, bearing, and nursing children* (1671) was the first of its kind. Sarah Jinner, author of *An Almanack for Prognostication* for the years 1658 to 1664, and other almanac writers, such as the midwife, Mary Holden, and

---

[1] Jews had come to England after the Norman Conquest and were expelled in 1290 under Edward I. After three hundred and fifty years of exile, they were allowed to return in 1640. The date of the petition indicates that the readmission must have proceeded rather slowly.

Mary Trye with her "Medicatrix, or the Woman Physician" (1675), tried to meet women's need for basic medical information. However, as early as 1622, Elizabeth Clinton, Countess of Lincoln had written a treatise entitled *The Countess of Lincole's Nurserie* in which she took exception to the custom of wet-nursing. Quoting examples from the Bible, she passionately argued for breast-feeding by the mother of the child. Elizabeth Cellier, midwife to the royal family during the reign of James II, published "A Scheme for the Foundation of a Royal Hospital, and Raising a Revenue of five or Six Thousand Pounds a year, by and for the Maintenance of a Corporation of skillful Midwives, of such Foundlings, or Exposed Children as shall be admitted therein" (n.d.) The pamphlet proposed to establish standards for midwives.[1]

After the Restoration, Royalist women petitioned for the return of their estates confiscated during the Commonwealth. As a rule, however, the phrasing of these legal writings indicates that they were penned by lawyers.

Throughout the seventeenth century, individual women began to record their recipes and home remedies. One such instance is Ellinor Fettiplace's cookery book written around 1604 but not published until 1986, which gives insight into cooking-lore of the early seventeenth century.[2] In 1683, *The young Cook's Monitor* appeared. Though published anonymously, it contained the instruction that the book was "for the use of my scholars only", indicating that some sort of schools for household management must have existed. Over a period of

---

[1] Henri Petter has kindly drawn my attention to the fascinating novel *The Seven Ages* by Eva Figes whose fictional representation of the plight of women gives an enlightening accompaniment to the period under discussion.

[2] Hilary Spurling, ed., *Ellinor Fettiplace's Receipt Book* 1604 (London: Penguin, 1986)

eleven years, Hannah Woolley (1623-1675) supplied her readers with books of recipes. Documents such as the account book of Joyce Jeffries of Ham Castle demonstrate that women could be successful managers. Yet the recognition that females were able to act in positions generally reserved to men, even to defend castles and write for publication led to no long term amelioration.

The uncertainties due to a religiously oscillating monarchy led to a need for minority groups under threat to assert themselves. Numerous literary contributions came from the Quakers, who were defining their sect and their doctrine.

According to the Quaker belief, all human beings are equal in the eyes of the Lord. Men and women, therefore, have the same rights as well as the same duties. Women were actually encouraged to preach and write. With her "Women's Speaking Justified" (1665), Margaret Fell-Fox, who herself wrote extensively, fervently advocated the axiom of women's equality. Despite their acceptance as men's equals, in itself a remarkable development, Quaker women directed their writings to the requirements of their religious community. Consequently, those texts which were not travel reports, petitions for gaoled brethren, or appeals for social improvement - such as prison reform - are conversion narratives in the Quakers' homiletic tradition rather than reappraisals of woman's lot.

The reign of Elizabeth I, then, as well as the period of the Civil Wars, had brought only temporary and ad hoc adjustment to the standing of women.

The Restoration, and in particular the re-opening of the London theaters, brought new possibilities. Actresses replaced boy actors, and women began to write and publish to support themselves. However, if they wanted to sell their product, they had to keep within the boundaries of literary and social etiquette.

A display of controversial ideas, especially anything we could now term feminist, would not have been commercially viable. As early as 1621, Mary Sidney Wroth, apparently in an attempt to pay for her debts, presented her "roman-à-clef", *The Countesse of Montgomeries Urania*, in part an extension of her uncle's *Arcadia*. The female protagonist, Pamphilia, "derives not only a sense of selfhood, but also creative power from her secret passions: reading, and, more significantly, writing."[1] This romance is "certainly concerned with women's sufferings; but the cause to which these are most often attributed is not patriarchal oppression, but men's inconstancy ... a timeless and irremedial feature of male nature" (Hackett p 50-51).

Aphra Behn, "seemingly the first English woman to live off the proceeds from her writings" (Smith, *Reason's Disciples* p 153) to some extent followed Mary Wroth's footsteps with her "chroniques scandaleuses". Known for her extravagant lifestyle, she openly referred to both male impotence and the delights of sexuality. Her writings reflect her own "libertine sexual ethic" (Lilley p 128). Furthermore, she presented her readers with "shockingly detailed descriptions" (Lilley, p 105) such as the brutal murder of the 'noble savage' in *Oroonoko* (1688), the "first novel to include condemnation of slavery" (Ferguson, *First Feminists*, p 143). In the preface to her play, *The Dutch Lover* (1673), Aphra Behn pointed out that men's great advantage over women was learning. While one admires Aphra Behn's forthright approach and her prolific output, all her heroines eventually bow to dominant males. "Behn's writings reverberate with echoes from the timelessness of romance" (Hobby, *Virtue*, p 97). Yet her "consistent premise is that the world would be a more loving and

---

[1] Helen Hackett, 'Yet Tell Me Some Such Fiction': Lady Mary Wroth's *Urania* and the 'Feminity' of Romance," *Women, Texts and Histories, 1575-1760*, eds. Clare Brant and Diane Purkiss (London: Routledge, 1992) p 51.

supportive place if it were run according to ... female beliefs. Her grim conclusion is that such a revolutionary change is impossible. All women can do is to make the best they can out of the status quo".(Hobby, *Virtue*, p 100) In her novels, she did describe deplorable aspects of the status of women, but by offering aspirations rather than concrete solutions, she contributed in only a minor way to a liberation of women.

At either end of the seventeenth century, Shakespeare and Congreve portrayed Beatrice and Millamant, women who professed a determination not to marry. Unlike Aphra Behn's flamboyant heroines, these creations of male playwrights defied conventions in a more restrained manner. However, after engaging in verbal duels in which they proved themselves as witty and shrewd as the heroes, each one submitted happily and, in the words of Millamant, "dwindle[d] into a wife".[1] In the case of Millamant, this occurred in the very year that Mary Astell was advocating spinsterhood with honour. The examples of Shakespeare and Congreve indicate the discrepancy between the expectations of a stage heroine speaking lines written by a man and the exigencies of a living authoress. Although men seemed to attribute to women a will for independence, it was in men's terms, and in the artificial environment of the stage.

Beatrice and Millamant valued autonomy and the freedom to speak, yet both were created by men. Congreve's heroine, though a century later than Shakespeare's, enjoyed no greater emancipation than did her predecessor. Outside the theater, though Mary Wroth hinted at a more liberal definition of women's expectations, there were few women writers in the early

---

[1] William Congreve, *The Way of the World*. 1700. " These articles subscribed, if I continue to endure you a little longer, I may by degrees dwindle into a wife." IV, 6.

seventeenth century who publicly expressed Beatrice's valiant desire to state terms before agreeing to marriage.

In his essay "Of Studies", Francis Bacon (1561-1626) chose to categorize studies under the heading of "delight", "ornament" and "ability":

> Studies serve for delight, for ornament, and for ability. Their chief use for delight is in privateness and retiring; for ornament, is in discourse; and for ability, is in the judgement and disposition of business.

In Bacon's day there was an automatic assumption, that any writings studied would have been written by a man. In the general introduction to her excellent anthology of women's writings, Charlotte Otten points out, that a woman going into print did, in fact, challenge "the theological and medical grounds that supported the inferiority of women - an inferiority that demanded silence" (p 1). However, while the literary merits of many women writing in the centuries after the death of Margery Kempe are indisputable, their proposals for improving women's standing remained so insubstantial that they must be catalogued as "ornament" or "delight". It was not until Mary Astell published her *Serious Proposal* in 1694 that "ability" commensurate with Margery Kempe's became manifest.

VIII MARY ASTELL 1666-1731

a)   Mary Astell's Claim for Further Consideration

She published the larger, and for me more relevant, parts of her work in the seventeenth century, but if her way of thinking belongs to the eighteenth, it is nonethless a product of what had been going on before. Even if most women retreated into silence after the Civil Wars, as a group they had proven that they were perfectly able to perform the duties normally executed by men - the very duties which one had hitherto assumed, could only be fulfilled by men.

Mary Astell is, therefore, an ideal person to consider when documenting both the preceding centuries and the beginning of the actual movement for the liberation of women. She was no bluestocking but she anticipated aspects of the argumentation typical of the eighteenth century feminists. Identifying her as a feminist, a term that only acquired its full meaning in our times, is debatable. However it seems justified to do so if we interpret the term according to the Oxford Advanced Learner's Dictionary: "feminism n. movement for recognition of the claims of women for rights (legal, political, etc.) equal to those possessed by men".

b)   Mary Astell - A Professional Writer

Despite the current intensity of research into the history of feminism, with the notable exception of Ruth Perry, there has been surprisingly little interest in Mary Astell.[1] The author of *A Serious Proposal to the Ladies, for the Advancement of Their True and Greatest Interest* and *Some Reflections Upon Marriage, Occasion'd by the Duke and Dutchess of Mazarine's Case; which is also considered* was possibly of minor importance to her contemporaries. Few of her private letters have been preserved and some of those were found by accident only. We are, therefore, in a situation reminiscent of the plight confronting a would-be biographer of Julian of Norwich or of Margery Kempe: we have little access to the author except through her own writings. As a result, twentieth-century scholars have to rely on documents written long after the death of the woman who has often been called the first feminist. Hilda Smith draws attention to a passage in John Evelyn's *Numismata* (1697) where the author refers to Mary Astell's *Serious Proposal* as an example of what "excellencies" women were capable of.[2] Some information can be found in the celebrated correspondence of her younger friend, Lady Mary Wortley Montagu, author of the *Embassy Letters* and militant fighter for the introduction of an inoculation against smallpox.[3] Her personal background was recorded in some detail in 1752 by John Ballard.[4] Mary Hays referred to

---

[1] Ruth Perry, *The Celebrated Mary Astell. An Early English Feminist* Chicago: University of Chicago Press, 1986.

[2] John Evelyn, *Numismata* 1667. p 256. EEB 276:6.

[3] Lady Mary Wortley Montagu, *Letters and Works*.ed. Lord Wharncliffe. 1837.

[4] George Ballard, *Memoirs of Several Ladies of Great Britain, Who Have Been Celebrated for Their Writings or Skill in the Learned Languages, Arts and Science.* (Oxford:1752) Gerritsen Collection, 54:150. pp 445-460.

Mary Astell's success in *Female Biography*.[1] Mary Pilkington outlined the life and work of Mary Astell in 1804.[2] In 1898, Harriet McIlquhan published articles on Mary Astell and her friendship with Lady Montagu.[3] Additional information appeared in 1916 when Florence Smith published her Ph.D. thesis.[4]

No portrait is known to exist. Mary Astell called herself "one to whom nature has not been overliberal".[5] The only other description of her appearance is found in a letter where a granddaughter of Lady Wortley Montagu said Mary Astell was "as far from fair and elegant as any old schoolmaster of her time" (Perry, p 23).

The fact that male writers of the time made reference to her *Serious Proposal to the Ladies* indicates that the work did make some impact. Ruth Perry draws attention to the fact that Richard Steele quoted large parts of the *Serious Proposal* in *The Ladies Library*, though he neglected to indicate the source (p 100). Hilda Smith points out that Daniel Defoe specified Mary Astell's work as an inspiration to his *Academy of Women* (Smith, *Reason's Disciples*, p 137). In addition, I tentatively suggest that with his title, *Modest Proposal*, Swift may have been mocking Mary Astell. Ruth Perry has pointed out that Mary Astell was ridiculed twice in three months in editions of *The Tatler* (p 228-229). The satirist on both occasions was either Richard Steele or

---

[1] Mary Hays, *Female Biography; or, Memoirs of Illustrious and Celebrated Women, of all Ages and Countries* 1802.

[2] Mrs. Mary Pilkington, "Mary Astell and Lady Mary Montagu". *Memoirs of Celebrated Female Characters* 1804.

[3] McIlquhan, Harriet. "Mary Astell a 17th Century Advocate for Women," *Westminster Review* 149(1898): pp 440-449.

[4] Florence Smith, *Mary Astell* (New York: Columbia University Press, 1916)

[5] John Norris, *Letters Concerning the Love of God, Between the Author of the Proposal to the Ladies and Mr. John Norris* (1694) Preface.

Jonathan Swift. Obviously, Mary Astell's project evoked interest. However, she did express disdain at the lack of support for her plan in *A Serious Proposal*, Part II. We may therefore assume that the disappointing lack of tangible patronage was the reason for her dropping the subject after 1700.

Mary Astell's writings were the first to deal expressly with feminist issues. Her outstandingly conservative views in matters of church and state probably protected her reputation and guaranteed a serious consideration of her ideas. As we have seen, restrospective evaluation came too late to preserve background information. As a result, Margaret Drabble did not add Mary Astell's name to the latest edition of the *Oxford Companion to English Literature*. It does, however, appear in Todd's and in Schlueters' lists. The *Feminist Companion to Literature in English* devotes half a page to her, but, rather than pay detailed homage to her plan for educating women, the editors refer to her as very witty and highly quotable.[1] Germaine Greer, author of *The Female Eunuch*, mentions Mary Astell.[2] However, the eminent twentieth century feminist cites from the anonymous *Essay in Defense of the Female Sex* (1696)[3] which, due to certain similarities in vocabulary, was attributed by George Ballard and others, to the author of *A Serious Proposal*. Florence Smith, however, doubts the authorship of Mary Astell and has suggested Judith Drake.

Hilda Smith wrote a chapter of *Reason's Disciples* on Mary Astell in 1982 and in 1986 Bridget Hill introduced and

---

[1] Virginia Blain, Patricia Cements, Isobel Grundy. eds. *The Feminist Companion to Literature in English* (London: B.T. Batsford 1990)

[2] Germaine Greer, *The Female Eunuch*. 1970. (London: Granada, 1971)

[3] Anon. *Essay in Defense od the Female Sex. In which are inserted the Characters of a Pedant, a Squire, a Beau, a Vertuoso, a Poetaster, a City-critick etc. In a Letter to a Lady, Written by a Lady* 1696.

edited some of the texts. The latest addition to the studies on Mary Astell is Ruth Perry's *The Celebrated Mary Astell* (1986).

As far as her character emerges from her texts, she seems to have been generally cheerful and to have pursued a moderate lifestyle, remaining unmarried and enjoying enough freedom to put into practice her belief that women could live independent of men. She entertained and was invited out, but also took pleasure in studying in peace, away from London's busy crowds.

Using all the available sources, we can assemble a scant outline of her early life.

In 1666 she was born into the family of a wealthy coal merchant in Newcastle-on-Tyne. Her mother, Mary Errington, was of Catholic stock, yet Mary Astell was brought up in the tradition of the Church of England and remained a devout and convinced Anglican throughout her life.

> I am a Christian then, and a member of the Church of England, not because I was Born in England, and Educated by Conforming Parents, but because I have, according to the very best of my Understanding, and with some application and industry, examin'd the Doctrine and Precepts of Christianity, the Reasons and Authority on which it is built.[1]

In her early youth she received some instruction in Logic, Mathematics and Philosophy possibly through her uncle, Ralph Astell. She enjoyed presenting rational arguments for the proof of her ideas as for instance when discussing the subjection of women to men:

---

[1] Mary Astell, *The Christian Religion as Profess'd by a Daughter of the Church of England* 1705. Bridget Hill, p 197.

But it will be said perhaps, that in I Tim. 2.13, etc. St Paul argues for the Woman's subjection from the Reason of things. To this I answer, that it must be confess'd that this (according to the vulgar Interpretation) is a very obscure place, and I shou'd be glad to see a Natural, and not a Forc'd Interpretation given of it by those who take it literally. Whereas if it be taken Allegorically, with respect to the Mystical Union between Christ and his Church, to which St Paul frequently accommodates the Matrimonial Relation, the difficulties vanish. For the Earthly Adam's being Form'd before Eve, seems as little to prove her Natural Subjection to him, as the Living Creatures, Fishes, Birds and Beasts being Form'd before them both, proves that Mankind must be subject to these Animals. (*R U M,* Preface)

This convincing argument is all the more powerful for being held in such gentle tones. She did not commit the mistake of later feminists who sometimes stretched the discussion ad absurdum by overloading flimsy arguments with exaggerated significance. The unadorned presentation of her reasoning is logical and most apposite. Two centuries later, Darwin presented his theory of evolution. In her observation and interpretation of the first two chapters of Genesis, was Mary Astell not almost anticipating Darwin's reasoning?

At the time of Mary Astell's early youth, Newcastle was a busy merchant town in an area where many affluent families lived. Celia Fiennes, the author of a contemporary travel diary, described entertainments such as exhibitions and theatres which attracted people from all over the north.[1] Contacts with other towns and their inhabitants were formed. Mary Astell's agile

---

[1] Celia Fiennes, *Travel Journals*. 1685-1703. ed. C. Morris. *The Journey of Celia Fiennes,* (London: 1947) pp 175-177.

mind must have profited from such an atmosphere which shaped her way of thinking.

Members of her extended family belonged to the landed gentry in the area. Possibly this early influence confirmed her Tory ideas.

When she was twelve years old, her father died.
We have little information about the next ten, formative years. It has been suggested that she grew up in an exclusively female household (Ruth Perry, p 59).

For unknown reasons, possibly because she had been orphaned, when she was about twenty two, she moved to Chelsea where she was supported by Bishop Sancroft, to whom she dedicated an early collection of her verse. He seems to have recognized her potential as a writer and helped her to get in contact with publishers such as Robert Wilkin, who published her books and later encouraged her to write political pamphlets. Both *A Serious Proposal to the Ladies* and *Some Reflections Upon Marriage* were published anonymously, but readers knew who had written them. It is interesting to note that rather than sign her name she identified herself as a woman, a "Lover of her Sex". This suggests that she did not seek personal fame but wanted to draw attention to the fact that the author was not a man.

After having settled in Chelsea she found access to a social level to which she did not actually belong by birth. Thanks to her high intelligence and erudition, she was admitted to aristocratic gatherings. All her closest friends were women, and, when she opened her own charity school in 1709, the teachers were all friends whom she had known for years. With one exception, all were unmarried and every one of them considered Mary Astell proof of the intellectual equality of men and women.

She was a firm believer in both monarchy and the Church of England. Although she suggested celibacy as an optional alternative to the institution of marriage, she accepted that within marriage there should be a hierarchy, with the husband's power similar to the absolute rule of a king. In her rational style, she logically concluded that one master was necessary and enough to keep a marriage or a state running smoothly. She continued writing until her death in 1731, but her role as advocate of change in the situation of women ended with *Some Reflections Upon Marriage*. As already explained, her proposition of a women's retreat was never realized. Although the author specifically mentioned that she wanted the place to be called religious retirement rather than monastery "to avoid giving offence to the scrupulous and injuducious, by names which tho' innocent in themselves have been abused by superstitious Practices" (*PROP*, p 150), financial support was not forthcoming. Possibly because this kind of establishment still smacked too much of the convent Mary Astell's *Proposal* failed to win church approval.

If, then, her most innovative theory was never realized, on what does her reputation rest?

Others had advocated education for women but never explicitly suggested liberation from the inevitablity of marriage, nor did they advocate celibacy. Celibate herself and supported by a group of like-minded women, Mary Astell demonstrated in both practice and theory what is termed, in the twentieth century, "sisterhood". Other women turned to her as an example of a thinker, intellectually the equal of men. I see her claims to fame in these two points: her advancing a viable alternative to becoming a wife and the concept of women as men's intellectual equals.

Her preoccupation with the status of women and with the development of a woman's mind in no way conflicted with her religious studies. Indeed, she saw the study of science as essential preparation for a life according to Christian principles: "we shall rescue our selves out of that woful incogitancy we have slipt into, awaken our sleeping Powers and make use of that reason which GOD has given us" (*PROP*, p 162).

Naturally, therefore, she was deeply concerned with the nature and origin of sin, which she defined as mental pain. In her correspondence with the Reverend John Norris, a late member of the Cambridge Platonists, she discussed this problem with intensity. The exchange of letters lasted over a period of ten months in 1692 and was published by John Norris under the title *Letters Concerning the Love of God* in 1695.

> Methinks there is all the reason in the World to conclude, That God is the only efficient Cause of all our Sensations; and you have made it clear as the Day; and it is equally clear from the Letter of the Commandment, That God is not only the Principal, but the sole Object of our Love: But the reason you assign for it, namely, Because he is the only efficient Cause of our Pleasure, seems not equally clear. (*LG*, Letter I, pp 2-3)

Julian of Norwich had no trouble equating divine and human love, not surprisingly, since she seems to have experienced very little of earthly love. In the late fourteenth century, the unknown author of "Pearl" blended the earthy and the sublime with impunity. Ernst Leisi has drawn attention to "das komplexe Ineinander von Spiritualität und Leiblichkeit bei

John Donne".[1] And indeed, the Dean of St Paul's metaphysical conceits depend on the interchange of sacred and profane love. In his poetic imagery, he used expressions of divine love when writing about his mistress and, more amazingly, wrote of carnal passion when describing his love of God.[2] Mary Astell, however, was unable to incorporate the idea of God as the origin of pleasure as well as pain into a plan of salvation, but was herself torn between the love of God on one hand and the love she felt for her fellow human beings on the other.

In her letters to John Norris she expressed deep unease that her pure love of God might be sullied by her compassion for the women who shared her hopes.

As will be seen, Mary Astell could write with an intensity of feeling which precludes accusations that this rational woman lacked heart. Her passion about her original ideas embraced the people who shared her commitment. These overlapping emotions confused the inexperienced young woman, who could have been in the process of self-definition. Possibly this bewilderment made her write to John Norris, asking him for help in disentangling her emotions.

> 'That we may seek Creatures for our own good, but not love them as our good', yet methinks 'tis too nice for common Practice; and through the Deception of our Senses, and hurry of our Passions, we shall be too apt to reckon that our good whose Absence we find uneasie to us. Be pleased therefore to oblige me with a Remedy for this Disorder, since what you have already writ has made a considerable Progress

---

[1] Ernst Leisi, *Paar und Sprache*. (1978; Heidelberg und Wiesbaden: Quelle und Meyer. 1993) p 68.

[2] John Donne, The Canonization.

> toward a Cure, but not quite perfected it.
> (*LG*, Letter 3, pp 50-51)

It was this letter which ultimately led scholars such as Ruth Perry and Bridget Hill to construe her love and gratitude towards like-minded women as explicit lesbian passion. But "Disorder", even taken in conjunction with her preferred lifestyle, need not be evidence of lesbian tendencies. Nowhere in his letters does John Norris interpret her words in this way. Furthermore, when discussing prejudice and error in *Serious Proposal*, Part II, she used the word "disorder" with no such connotation. Therefore, I see little justification for the scholars' equating the word with homosexuality.

In the preface to *Letters Concerning the Love of God*, Mary Astell explained the dedication to Lady Catherine Jones, one of the Chelsea group.

> For though none can be less fond of Dedications, or has so little Ambition to be known to those who are called great, yet out of Regard I owe to the Glorious Author of all Perfection I cannot but pay a very great Respect to one who so nearly resembles him ... One whom now we have truly stathe [sic] the Measures, I may venture to say, I love with the greatest Tenderness, for all must love her who have any Esteem for Unfeigned Goodness, who value an early Piety and eminent Vertue.

She went on to speak of a devotion "so fervent and so prudent, so equally composed of Heat and Light"; she described the "Seraphick Flames" felt when praying next to this epitome of virtue and beauty; she deplored the fact that her expressions were "too flat", the colours "too dead to draw such a lovely Piece!".

In a public dedication, Mary Astell would hardly have used flamboyantly emotional language, that could be interpreted as a shameful "Disorder". Clearly, the problem outlined in her letter to John Norris, was nothing more than a scruple about her irreconcilable feelings in the process of finding the perfect love of God.

If an individual steps outside conventional ways, different rules apply. Mary Astell had no parents to honour, no husband to cherish, and no children to pour her love on.

According to twentieth century psychology, she had to find a substitute. An obvious possibility would be for her to depend on those individuals who supported her fervent ideas and emulated her lifestyle.

Convenient and attractive as the idea may be, slotting Mary Astell and certain of her writings into a file labelled Lesbian Literature is not justifiable. Furthermore, debates about her sexual preference have no more relevance to her literary output than has the discussion of whether Margery Kempe was or was not a true mystic.

Some researchers see her as a member of a marginalized group, even as the first feminist. Politically a conservative, she challenged tradition; advocating and practicing celibacy, she supported hierarchy within marriage. Mary Astell defies cataloguing. Moreover, her biography as well as her writings pose some questions. Why did she leave the north of England? Where did her critical attitude to men originate?

My opinion is that she was a highly emotional person and committed herself thoroughly to everything she undertook. She felt deep unhappiness about the situation of women who had, during the Civil Wars, demonstrated a capacity for independence and then been pushed back into subservience by the returning heroes.

Where powerful feelings were touched, she wrote passionately. Yet, her inclusion of "Logic and Natural Sciences" in a curriculum for women demonstrated her respect for rational order. The clash between the emotional and the rational could have created the frustration that made her write. If so, deprivation led to creativity and the outburst of her feelings culminated in her two works concerning the lot of women at the time.

c) Mary Astell's Contribution to Literature and the Status of Women

Although at least nine of Mary Astell's works were published, only three are relevant to my thesis. Moreover, although she continued to write, after 1700 she no longer concerned herself with the standing of women.[1] *A Serious Proposal for the Ladies*, Part I was published in 1694. *The Second Part of the Proposal to the Ladies* was written in 1697 and appeared in the same year, together with the first part, as one edition. This work has been called "the earliest and most impressive ... to concentrate on women's position within society" and is a fervent argument for admitting women to the "tree of knowledge" (Smith, *Reason's*

---

[1] For a complete list of Mary Astell's writings, the reader is referred to Hill. I have been able to peruse Mary Astell's works in their entirety on microfilm only. For convenience's sake I have opted to quote from Bridget Hill's excellent and almost complete edition of *A Serious Proposal*, (3rd edition corrected, 1696). (Page numbers refer to her edition). As for *A Serious Proposal*, Part II, *Some Reflections Upon Marriage*, and *Letters Concerning the Love of God*, my quotations are from the University Microfilms International copies.

A Serious Proposal part II: EEB 1414:49

Some Reflections Upon Marriage: EEB 1029:10

Letters Concerning the Love of God: EEB 231:6

Disciples, p 117). Her third opus, *Some Reflections Upon Marriage*, was triggered by the notorious case of the Duke and Duchess of Mazarine. Her empathy with the unfortunate woman, trapped by society in a situation she was not equipped to mitigate, led Mary Astell to use this specific predicament to substantiate and intensify her earlier apprehension about the traditional fate of women. Furthermore, she felt justified in repeating her warning against "the dangers of an ill Education and unequal Marriage" (*PROP,* p 4).

Mary Astell's letters to John Norris and his answers were published by her correspondent in 1695 under the title *Letters Concerning the Love of God Between the Author of the Proposal to the Ladies and Mr. John Norris, wherein his Discourse shewing That it ought be entire and exclusive of all other Loves is further declared and justified.* In some instances, this correspondence can provide additional information on her character and personality.

Because, as the editors of the *Feminist Companion to Literature in English* have pointed out, Mary Astell is eminently quotable, there is a danger that a general reader will know her merely as a writer of epigrammatic snippets. From the length of my quotations it must be clear that I value her prose for its rhythm as well as its balanced development.

A Serious Proposal, Part I, is primarily the argumentation for a retreat where women could spend their time learning rather than fritter it away according to social convention. Almost as a parallel within the same text, Mary Astell dealt with the restrictions imposed on women. Her suggested alternatives did not propose material changes in a woman's lot. Rather, she wanted to change society's perception of that lot. She challenged women to "surpass men as much in Vertue and Ingenuity, as ... in

Beauty" (*PROP*, p 139). She admonished her female readers not to have degrading thoughts of their own worth, but to build up self-esteem and avoid "being Cyphers in the World" (*PROP*, p 143). To use Germaine Greer's words, she saw that a woman "could not begin by changing the world, but by reassessing herself" (p 14).

A Serious Proposal, Part II, may have been written because the requisite approval and financial support for her plans, called for in Part I, had failed to materialize. In this supplement to her first book, Mary Astell substantiated her original claim that, given the necessary opportunities, women were intellectually equal to men. Ideas were repeated and fleshed out where she felt additional arguments were needed or where observation of the initial reaction to her ideas made further explanation necessary.

Some Reflections Upon Marriage deals specifically with women's relationships to men within or without marriage. Here, she addressed herself more practically to possibilities open to spinsters. In no other work did she treat this concern so fully. As in *Serious Proposal*, she came to the conclusion that education was an absolute necessity. Furthermore, she stressed the importance of a sound instruction rather than a smattering of learning. Superficial knowledge, she argued, would make "Women vain and assuming, and instead of correcting encrease their Pride" (*PROP*, p 167). Once women were able to apply reason to their actions and thoughts, they would see the importance of independence and equality.

The number of copies sold indicates that *Serious Proposal* was the more widely read at the time.[1] However, Hilda Smith

---

[1] *A Serious Proposal*, first published in 1694, had run to four editions by 1701, whereas the fourth edition of *Some Reflections Upon Marriage* was not published until 1730.

considers *Some Reflections Upon Marriage* the more feminist and modern piece of writing because the author indicated some doubts about the justification of male hegemony (Smith, *Reason's disciples* p 137). Possibly *Some Reflections* went too far for a seventeenth-century audience; people were not yet ready for either such dramatic rethinking of the role of women or for any evaluation of educational policy. Mary Astell's specific suggestion of an institution for women attracted attention because it was not basically new, for with the abolition of convents, an important possibility for educating women had been lost. Furthermore, a retreat for unmarriageable women had disappeared. Mary Astell's proposal would have revived both ideas, which she presented in a fashion she considered appropriate to her time.

Mary Astell wrote all her works dealing with the issue of the standing of women before 1700. This date happens to coincide with the arbitrarily chosen end to the period of my considerations. As early as 1694, Mary Astell was already anticipating the blue-stocking movement. As an Anglican, she was bold in wanting to give new life to retreats for women that were reminiscent of convents. Mary Astell's vision was amalgamating proven solutions from the past with practicable notions that did not begin to materialize until well after 1700, and it is justifiable to say that she bridged the gap between the centuries. She must be considered a significant contributor to the development of self-esteem in women.

Mary Astell has to be viewed in the context of her contemporaries. As I pointed out earlier, literacy among women increased significantly during the seventeenth century. They became a reading public. Women began to write for women.

Bathsua Makin, who wrote an essay propagating education for women in 1673, ran a highly respected school for girls in London and was of the opinion that the time spent on teaching women how to please men could better be used in shaping their spiritual values.[1] Anna Maria van Schurman's "The Learned Maid or, whether a Maid may be a Scholar" was translated from the Dutch in 1659.[2] Ruth Perry has pointed out the perfectly shaped rhetoric of Anna Maria van Schurman's book which, she says, "displays delight in all forms of scholastic discourse" (p 15). It was read widely in England and could very well have influenced Mary Astell who, as will be seen, greatly enjoyed writing finely crafted texts. The Dutch author demonstrated pleasure in intellectual exercise, but argued no real social changes. The subjects taught at Bathsua Makin's school were the traditional ones: Religion, Manners, Arts and Tongues. To a certain extent Mary Astell's proposal reflected the modern ideas on education that Bathsua Makin had put forward twenty years earlier. However, where Bathsua Makin, like Anna Maria van Schurman, was prepared to debate whether or not a woman had an intellect, Mary Astell took that issue for granted and concentrated on the possibilities of using innate intelligence. Although the basic desire for a change in the educational policy of women is evident in their writings, neither Bathsua Makin nor Anna Maria van Schurman went as far as Mary Astell.

Aphra Behn, best-known for her novel *Oroonoko* (1688), wrote in order to be able to pay her debts. Elizabeth Elstob was known as the "Anglo-Saxon scholar". Another writer of the time, Damaris Masham, concerned herself mostly with theological and

---

[1] Bathsua Makin, *Essay to Revive the Antient Education of Gentlewomen* (1673)

[2] Anna Maria Van Schurman, *The Learned Maid or, whether a Maid may be a Scholar* (1659)

psychological questions. All these writers consciously or otherwise reflected different aspects of progress in the development towards a liberation of women. Mary Astell alone, however, clearly foreshadowed the bluestocking movement of the following century.

She dealt with the hampering effect of tradition on women's lives. She felt that in many ways to follow tradition was contrary to women's interests.

> Thus Ignorance and a narrow Education lay the Foundation of Vice, and Imitation and Custom rear it up. Custom, that merciless torrent that carries all before it, and which indeed can be stemmed by none but such as have a great deal of Prudence and a rooted Vertue. (*PROP*, p 147)

Furthermore, she deplored the lack of possibilities for education. Unlike her forerunners, she did not stop to lament the situation and blame men for the miserable state of affairs. While accusing men, basically, of willfully keeping women in ignorance, she attributed a share of responsibility to women's own "false Judgements, unreasonable desires and Expectations" (*RUM*, p 55):

> If from our Infancy we are nurs'd up in Ignorance and Vanity; are taught to be Proud and Petulant, Delicate and Fantastick, Humorous and Inconstant, 'tis not strange that the ill effects of this Conduct appear in all the future Actions of our Lives." (*PROP*, p 144)

Although her sympathies were obviously on the women's side, she successfully avoided extremism, refusing to condemn all men as a matter of principle. Her contacts with John Norris and Bishop Sancroft prove that she, in fact, appreciated an exchange of ideas with men on an intellectual level. It was patriarchal men on whom she poured her wrath; men who opposed women's desire to acquire knowledge outside their traditional domain; men who subjected women and kept them within the artificial boundaries that had been assigned to them by custom. Without giving women a chance for improvement, such men accused them of being wanton.

> Women are from their very Infancy debar'd those Advantages, with the want of which they are afterwards reproached, and nurs'd up in those Vices which will hereafter be upbraided to them. (*PROP*, p 143)

She held men accountable for this state.

> That therefore Women are unprofitable to most, and a plague and dishonour to some men is not much to be regretted on account of the Men, because 'tis the product of their own folly, in denying them the benefits of an ingenuous and liberal Education, the most effectual means to direct them into, and to secure their progress in the ways of Vertue. (*R U M*, p 145)

Since Mary Astell considered ignorance the cause of all sin, education was particularly important for the devout Christian.

> And seeing it is Ignorance, either habitual or actual, which is the cause of all sin, how are they like to escape this that are bred up in that? (*PROP*, p 144)

She realized that the ideological concept of the role of women had to be changed before any practical modifications could take place. Educating women and enabling them to take their destiny into their own hands was the first and most important step.

There was no way, she argued, that men could reasonably oppose education of women, because it was evident that mothers had all the opportunities for giving form and season to the tender mind, to "make or mar" the character of the child.

In no uncertain terms she suggested changing the traditional way women spent their lives:

> For shame let's abandon that Old, and therefore one wou'd think, unfashionable employment of chasing Butter flies and Trifles! No longer drudge on in the beaten road of Vanity and Folly, which so many have gone before us, but dare to break the enchanted Circle that custom has plac'd us in, and scorn the vulgar way of imitating all the Impertinencies of our Neighbours. Let us learn to pride ourselves in something more excellent than the invention of a Fashion; And not entertain such degrading thought of our own worth, as to imagine that our Souls were given us only for the service of our Bodies, and that the best improvement we can make of these, is to attract the Eyes of Men. We value them too much, and ourselves too little, if we place any part ot our desert in their Opinion; and don't think our selves capable of Nobler Things than the pityful Conquest of some worthless heart. (*PROP*, p 141)

Already in 1694 she was anticipating what she was to express more fully in her *Reflections Upon Marriage*.

Would-be wives, women who were never taught that they "should have a higher Design than to get ... a husband" (*R U M,* p 66), were warned that in marriage they would have a high price to pay. A woman gaining a husband

> puts her self intirely in his Power, leaves all that is dear to her, her Friends and Family, to espouse his Interests and follow his Fortune, and makes it her Business and Duty to please him! (*R U M*, p 46)

In view of such sacrifices Mary Astell considered it far wiser to stay single than to accept, as prescribed by custom, a "Monarch for Life" (*R U M,* p 32), a commitment which would possibly lead to an unhappy future:

> A Woman that thinks twice might bless her self and say, is this the Lord and Master to whom I am to promise Love, Honour and Obedience? (*R U M*, p 33)

The consequences of a rash decision were depicted in vivid detail.

> To be yoak'd for Life to a disagreeable Person and Temper, to have Folly and Ignorance tyrannize over Wit and Sense; to be contradicted in every thing one does or says, and bore down not by Reason but Authority; to be denied ones [sic] most innocent desires for no other cause, but the Will and Pleasure of an absolute Lord and Master, whose follies a Woman with all her Prudence cannot hide, and whose Commands she cannot but despise at the same time she obeys them, is a misery none can have a just idea, but those who have felt it. (*R U M*, p 4)

Apart from illustrating her contempt for men, this passage exemplifies the intensity of Mary Astell's engagement. So keenly did she identify with the women in bondage that she forgot that she herself had never had the actual experience. But further on she softened her discouraging descriptions of the matrimonial yoke by explicitly pointing out that the institution of marriage was created by the endless sapience of God.

> It is the Institution of Heaven, the only Honourable way of continuing Mankind, and far be it from us to think that there could have been a better than infinite Wisdom has found out for us. (*R U M*, p 9)

All the way through, her writing reflects the conservative character of a staunch believer in Tory and High Church ideas. The intensity of her belief can be illustrated by the following passage, in which she reminded the reader that Jesus himself

> punctually observ'd the innocent usages of the Jewish Church, tho' in many instances the reason of the Command ceas'd as to him, yet he wou'd obey the letter to avoid giving offence and to set us an admirable pattern of obedience. (*PROP*, p 156)

She demonstrated that even for her, the declared rationalist, in church matters duty clearly took precedence over reason. In *Some Reflections* she pointed out that "The Christian Institution of Marriage provides the best that may be for Domestic Quiet and Content, and for the Education of Children" (p 11). When she came to discussing the status of the woman in marriage, she clearly assigned superiority to the man, thus transferring her loyal feelings for the throne onto the level of the family:

by right or wrong the Husband gains his will. For Covenants between Husband and wife, like Laws in an Arbitrary Government, are of little Force, the Will of the Sovereign is all in all. (*R U M*, p 39)

No iconoclast, she even more explicitly enforced her principle later in the text:

She then who Marrys ought to lay it down for an indisputable Maxim, that her Husband must govern absolutely and intirely, and that she has nothing else to do but to Please and Obey. (*R U M*, p 59)

However, while accepting the husband's superior rights, Mary Astell complained about the moral double standard in a marriage where the woman "has the much harder bargain ... and neither Law nor custom affords her that redressment which a man obtains" (*R U M,* p 28).

In spite of a general wariness about the institution as such, she was ready to consider a happy marriage, where both partners were "equal in Birth, Education and Fortune" (*R U M*, p 105) a possible option to celibacy. She was aware of the biological fact that if it is "not good for a Woman to Marry, ... so there's an end of Human Race" (*R U M*, p 93). Furthermore, she was ready to concede that happiness in marriage was actually conceivable "provided we take but competent Care, Act like wise Men and Christians, and acquit our selves as we ought" (*R U M*, p 10).

She stressed the importance of carefully matching marriage partners, insisting on their spiritual qualities:

> What then is to be done? How must a Man chuse, and what Qualities must encline a Woman to accept, that so our Marry'd couple may be as happy as that State can make them? This is no hard Question: let the Soul be principally considered, and regard had in the first Place to a Good Understanding, a Vertuous Mind, and in other respects let there be as much equality as may be. If they are good Christians and of suitable Tempers all will be well. (*R U M*, p 42)

The most innovative of her ideas was that women actually did have a say in major decisions of their lives. Marriage was one valid option which they could accept or waive. Having chosen marriage in principle, they could reject undesirable suitors. However, as Mary Astell repeatedly pointed out, while a man could search for a partner, the woman had to sit and passively wait.

More important, she claimed that for those who declined marriage there were other possibilities than to become the "superanuated [sic] spinster" with no practical purpose in society. She dismissed the view that an unmarried woman must inevitably be useless. First of all, to be an old maid should no longer carry the stigma of failure but could become the conscious expression of awareness that women were able to perform far more than the traditional duties. Being married then would no longer be the only way for a woman to qualify for social recognition. Single women were as important to society as mothers. Mary Astell postulated spinsterhood with honour against the traditional opinion that an unmarried woman was a burden to society.

> Nor will Knowledge lie dead upon their hands who have no children to Instruct; the whole World is a single Lady's Family, her opportunities of doing good are not lessen'd but increase'd by her being unconfin'd. Particular Obligations do not contract her Mind, but her Benefice moves in the largest Sphere. (*PROP*, p 178)

To those unwilling to give up their independence, she suggested alternatives. Her analysis had already identified lack of education as a source of women's despondency. Now the disease had been diagnosed, a remedy must be applied. In her *Serious Proposal* she outlined a pious, decent institution where women could acquire the tools necessary for them to take responsibility for their own destiny.

Her *Serious Proposal*, was to erect a retreat for those

> who are convinc'd of the emptiness of Earthly enjoyments, who are sick of the vanity of the world and its impertinences, may find more substantial and satisfying entertainment, and need not be confined to what they justly loathe. (*PROP*, p 150)

After presenting the readers with a list of the inconveniences of living in the world, she suggested "a convenient and blissful recess from the noise and trouble, the folly and temptation of the World", a "Type and Antepast of Heav'n" where they would suffer "no other confinement, but to be kept out of the road of sin" (*PROP*, pp 150-151) - an ideal option for those who did not wish to grasp marriage as a last, if desperate, resort. Admission entailed no vows or irrevocable obligations, but the entry fee of five hundred pounds would exclude all but "Persons of Quality" (*PROP*, pp 150-151). Each member could define the length of her stay; some might remain in this protected seclusion; others would leave once they had "the perfect government of themselves, and therefore rule according to Reason not Humour, consulting the good of the Society, not their own arbitrary sway" (*PROP*, p 158). There was "no other tye but the Pleasure, the Glory and Advantage of this blessed Retirement" (*PROP*, p 158).

Mary Astell based her proposal on the assumption of intellectual equality between men and women. Her aim was to invite women to participate actively in the world of education that had for so long been unjustly monopolized by men. In her retreat, a Christian life style and the study of logic were to be the underlying principles. According to Mary Astell, all sincere students of logic would inevitably find perfection in Christianity. She considered it a woman's duty to form her own true idea of Christian ethics, confident that there was no conflict between intellectual freedom and religious conformity. In a Catholic community such a syllabus would have been seen as invitation to violate the vow of obedience. Only a superficial reading of *A Serious Proposal* could give rise to accusations of popishness. But, as I pointed out, her plan was doomed to failure because, to casual readers, it recalled an image of the Roman Catholic convent as an institution. She pointed out that it "cannot be thought sufficient that Women shou'd but just know whats Commanded and what Forbid, whithout being inform'd of the Reasons why"(*PROP II*, p 205). And since "Religion never appeared in it's true Beauty, but when it is accompanied with Wisdom and Discretion" (*PROP*, p 152) the importance of acquiring this wisdom through education became even more obvious. More than two hundred years earlier, Julian of Norwich pronounced reason "*pe* hyghest gyfte that we haue receyved". At the same time she referred to it as "growndyd in kynd", implying that the power of reasoning was given to every human being. For her proposed retreat, Mary Astell argued along the same lines:

> God does nothing in vain, he gives no Power or Faculty which he has not allotted to some proportionate use, if therefore he has given to Mankind a Rational Mind, every individual Understanding ought to be employ'd in somewhat worthy of it. (*PROP* II, p 123)

Given opportunity to broaden their minds, women would be perfectly able to look after themselves; marriage would cease to appear the inevitable lot of every woman who did not wish to be a burden to society. Superannuated spinsters and female slaves would become things of the past.[1] The foundation of the retreat, however, would be religious. This "Happy Society", this "one Body whose Soul is love, animating and informing it",

---

[1] It is interesting to note that Mary Astell, while accusing men of holding women slaves, did not mention the problem of the slave-trade.

would lead a frugal life, "perpetually breathing forth it self in flames of holy desires after GOD and acts of Benevolence to each other" (*PROP*, p 157).

Mary Astell assumed what had been officially declared at the beginning of the Middle Ages - that women just like men had souls. However, she argued, not only did both men and women have souls, they had intelligent souls and it would in fact be wrong to forbid the use of this God-given faculty.

Mary Astell envisaged a protected retreat in which women could acquire both intellectual skills and self awareness. Reading idle novels and romances was to be replaced by the study of "Des Cartes, Malebranche and others" (*PROP*, p 155) in their original language. Protected by "this holy Roof" women would be able to "quit the Chat of insignificant people for an ingenious Conversation; the froth of flashy Wit for real Wisdom; idle tales for instructive discourses" (*PROP*, p 150).

In this environment of mutual tolerance "Censure will refine into friendly Admonition, all Scoffing and offensive Railleries will be abominated and banish'd" (*PROP*, p 157). "Ingenious Diversions, Musick particularly" would not only be permitted but required as they would "refresh the Body without enervating the Mind" (*PROP*, p 157). Mary Astell promised that the members of the community would "begin to throw off ... old Prejudices and smile on *p*em [sic] as antiquated Garbs" (*PROP II*, p 12).

Thus qualified, women could make a rational choice about their individual contribution to society. Mary Astell's own consistent application of choice can be illustrated by the quotation (above, p 145) where she discusses her standing as a Christian and member of the Church of England.

I consider the proposed re-evaluation of the significance of celibate women the most important of Mary Astell's ideas. Without a change of perception there could be no true freedom of choice for women. Why should women choose to stay single if their lot would then be worse than in an unhappy marriage, and grant them no socially acknowledged position or purpose?

Mary Astell - the extreme conservative - was cerainly making inflammatory claims in stating that women could take decisions and that they could contribute to society in more ways than by populating nurseries and adorning dinner-tables. Such assertions have earned her the title of "First Feminist". But writing in the pre-Enlightenment climate, she was aware that she was risking the damnation of her dream in its very proposal, which was, basically, a questioning of tradition. Therefore, when it came to actual recommendations, she was most circumspect and took great care not to seem a radical reformer.

Her diplomacy can be called pragmatic - pragmatic in the definition of William James, who claimed that abstract new ideas have to harmonize with our other experience and accepted ideas.[1] To all appearance, in *Serious Proposal*, Part I, she spoke against "pragmaticalness" (p 164), but of course she was using it in the older sense of something meddlesome or dogmatic.

Further proof of her diplomacy can be seen in her dedications. Where the original *Serious Proposal* was inscribed to all women, she dedicated the second part to Princess Anne of Denmark.[2] The later Queen Anne, possibly Ballard's "certain great lady", who seemed so much in favour of the idea of a

---

[1] William James, *Pragmatism* 1907.

[2] Bridget Hill seems to have overlooked the significance of Mary Astell's changing her dedication. In "The First Feminist", Hill printed the dedication to Princess Anne of Denmark, before part I of *A Serious Proposal*.

religious retreat that she intended to donate £10,000 for the realization of the project (Ballard, p 446 and Perry, p 188).

Her own concept of logic led Mary Astell to develop strategies that anticipated our twentieth-century definition by more than two hundred years. She was able to suggest changes in ways that seemed to avoid upsetting the existing social framework.

Furthermore, Mary Astell was realistic enough to address only persons of higher levels of society. On the one hand, the planned retreat would simply not be possible without some substantial financial support. On the other, she clearly saw that it was too early to include those women who had only just become literate and needed time to adjust to the realisation that now they were actually able to digest ideas in an unadulterated form. Because she genuinely felt for the cause, she took no risks that might endanger the eventual efficacy of her proposal.

Another demonstration of her good sense is to be seen in her use of outspoken epithets. All through her works she employed a specific strategy. After bluntly stating some incisive opinion she would soften the blow by reworking the same statement from different viewpoints. However, the impact of what was first said remained. By attacking and then repeating the attack in a more moderate version, she manipulated her adversaries. In a section discussing the relationship between husband and wife, Mary Astell used terms "Superior" and "Inferior" and likened the man to "the most absolute Tyrant" (*R U M*, p 47). On the following page, she almost excused him:

> But how can a Man respect his Wife when he has a contemptible Opinion of her and her Sex? When from his own Elevation he looks down on them as void of Understanding, and full of Ignorance and

> Passion, so that Folly and a Woman are equivalent Terms with him? (*R U M*, p 49)

However, rare exceptions to her pragmatically deferential demeanor occurred when she attacked the "Superior Sex".

> Have not all the great Actions that have been perform'd in the World been done by Men? Have not they founded Empires and overturn'd them? Do not they make Laws and continually repeal and amend them? Their vast Minds lay Kingdoms wast, no bounds or measures can be prescrib'd to their Desires. War and Peace depend on them, they form Cabals and have the Wisdom and Courage to get over all the Rubs which may lie in the way of their desired Grandeur. What is it they cannot do? They make Worlds and ruine them, form Systems of universal nature and dispute eternally about them; their Pen gives worth to the most trifling Controversie; nor can a fray be inconsiderable if they have drawn their Swords in't. All that the wise Man pronounces is an Oracle, and every Word the Witty speaks a Jest. (*R U M*, p 58-59)

Here Mary Astell is openly ridiculing men. That she should use irony seems to be in contradiction to her otherwise submissive approach. However, as has just been pointed out, passion about the plight of women occasionally did sway the calm and logical presentation of her thoughts. The Penguin *Dictionary of Literary Terms* traces the development of irony:

> We can see Milton working his way towards using it in his fashion in Areopagitica (1644), and Dryden beginning to employ it more and more in his satires. The increasing pleasure taken in parody and

burlesque suggests a growing awareness of the possible scope of irony. Then at the beginning of the 18th c. irony becomes fashionable. (Cuddon p 340)

Mary Astell was clearly part of that literary tradition. Yet her treating the subject by hitting at male supremacy through a list of specific examples rather than resorting to unsubstantiated whining is highly effective. In addition, by employing irony, she was showing men that she was able to turn their own literary weapon against them.

In *Serious Proposal*, Part II, Mary Astell dealt at length with her ideas on style, denigrating

> what Thought was Crude, or ill exprest, what Reasoning weak, what passage superfluous, where we were flat and dull, where extravagant and vain. (p 184)

Her texts show her to have followed her own advice closely. The generally sparse nature of her texts, trimmed of frivolities, effectively set off her selectively vivid passages to produce cogent arguments. Her address was diplomatic yet her style outspoken and her punch-phrases admirably coined. Quotations from the Bible illustrate Mary Astell's conviction of its relevance to her cause. Embellished with French, Latin, and Italian phrases, her texts demonstrate the erudition of their author. She argued with a clarity that proves a good sense for important points as well as an impressive ability to digest theoretical advice and re-present it appropriately for her reading public. The pleasure she must have experienced in using her active mind when proffering her organized thoughts in writing transmits itself to the reader. All through her texts her delight in using as well as in displaying her eminent intelligence is obvious. However, she did not let this personal enjoyment interfere with what was most important to her - the plight of women and her proposal for improving their lot.

My choice of quotations from the works of Mary Astell, illustrate, I hope, more than her "quotability". They demonstrate her engagement for the cause, her deference towards existing social structures and her gift of handling vocabulary and style appropriately. Furthermore, they exemplify both her ability in reasoning and her detached passion. Although she did on occasion lose her calm when writing directly about men, more often she listened to her own advice. In the following passage she succeeded in mercilessly presenting an abhorrent fate without actually accusing the originators of the deplorable state - men.

> Quite terrified with the dreadful Name Old Maid, which yet none but Fools will reproach her with, nor any wise Woman be afraid of; to avoid this terrible Mormo, and the scoffs that are thrown on superanuated [sic] Virgins, she flies to some dishonourable Match as her last, tho' much mistaken Refuge, to the disgrace of her Family and her own irreparable Ruin. And now let any Person of Honour tell me, if it were not richly worth some thousand Pounds, to prevent all this mischief, and the having an idle Fellow, and perhaps a race of beggarly Children to hang on him and to provide for? (*PROP*, p 169)

Her desire, to treat opponents fairly due to her strongly religious inclination, resulted in an effective presentation of her cause. Her selection of apposite vocabulary reflected her awareness of the intelligence and receptivity of her readers. From her choice of individual words to her overall organisation of argument - at all stylistic levels - she was consciously directing her proposal to any woman ready to accept her invitation, as well as to all possible patrons, be they men or women.

"Her work combined Christian faith with a sophisticated rationalist construction in a system that paralleled Descartes's 'Discourse on Method' " (Smith, *Reason's Disciples* p 119).

IX MARGERY KEMPE - THE FIRST ENGLISH FEMINIST

A close reading of Margery Kempe's *Book* revealed an unexpected achievement. Many women have lamented their fate, yet here was one who defined and overcame constraints. If such a desire for independence found literary expression at the beginning of the fifteenth century, what further evidence of feminist awareness was to be discovered in the succeeding years?

Despite a careful sifting of diaries, letters, and more public prose writings, I found no authoress of the fifteenth, sixteenth, or early seventeenth century who seemed a worthy successor to Margery Kempe's and her intransigent fight. Not until I studied Mary Astell's books dealing with feminist issues, was I to find any documents of equivalent significance.

By using the same technique as I employed when comparing and contrasting Julian of Norwich and Margery Kempe, I hope to justify the result of my research - the conclusion that Margery Kempe must, in fact, be considered a forerunner of today's movement for the liberation of women.

Having approached Mary Astell and her work largely from a twentieth century viewpoint, I now want to consider her contribution to feminism measured against the achievement of her predecessor - Margery Kempe. Especially when held against the contemporary *Book of Showings to the Anchoress Julian of Norwich*, we have seen that *The Book of Margery Kempe* articulates an amazingly modern, feminist outlook. By subjecting Margery Kempe and Mary Astell to a comparative scrutiny, I hope to demonstrate that despite their obvious contrasts, they did address basically the same need: a fundamental desire for independence.

Preoccupied with herself and backward-looking, Margery Kempe constrasts with Mary Astell, who assessed the world outside herself, and offered serious proposals for the future. While the *Book of Margery Kempe* exposes aspects of the almost exhibitionist character of its author, Mary Astell hid behind the formality of a literary tradition that did not let emotion distort reasoned argument.

Mary Astell, aware of the importance of style, content, and presentation, stressed that "order makes everything Easie, Strong and Beautiful" (*PROP II*, p 146). While obviously enjoying her gifts, she consciously wrote for an audience whose frame of mind she assessed constantly. Her discursive prose can entertain and amuse but its purpose was didactic. Had Margery Kempe been totally indifferent to an audience, she would not have fought against all odds in her determination to get her life-story written. At length, the *Book* was created, the concrete product of an intuitive achievement. Margery Kempe's narrative conveys scene and experience with a veracity that demands identification on the part of the reader.

Both authors, one living at the close of the Middle Ages and the other after the Restoration, were representative of their day. The colloquial style of Margery Kempe's reminiscences, evoking the spontaneity found in parts of the Mystery Plays, contrasts with Mary Astell's literary and consciously constructed arguments.

Identifying with all women, Mary Astell saw herself as their advocate; Margery Kempe, finally secure in herself, concentrated on her personal fulfillment. Her stubborn character and her belief in the importance of her travails drove her to find scribes, record her life, and overcome the threat of obliteration.

Mary Astell was able both to study and to digest what had been going on in the preceding centuries. Thanks to her education, she imbibed the full spectrum of conflicting arguments and deliberately demonstrated her erudition. Aware of the heroic feats of women, even though contemporary males in the post-Civil War period were demanding that women resume the mantle of the "weaker vessel", she knew the potential of her sisters and was able to suggest practicable improvements.

Although the author of *The Book of Margery Kempe* may have molded her life to a certain extent on stories she had heard about continental woman mystics, she presumably had no literary model for her work. Yet it was illiterate Margery Kempe who produced the first known autobiography in English.

In order to be able to substantiate my claim that both these women's achievements are milestones in the evolution of feminism, I have had to look behind the outward form of their works. A number of aspects may become important when defining the respective authors' positions in the anticipation of the feminist movement.

The *Book* was lost for about five hundred years and did not appear in print until 1940. Mary Astell's work never actually disappeared, but the rather sporadic comments over the centuries indicate that an initial interest in her writings dwindled; only recently have her ideas become the object of more research. Interestingly, studies of Margery Kempe were published by men and women alike; with the exception of George Ballard, the commentators on Mary Astell, "The First Feminist", have been women. The disparity may have to do with the fact that feminist studies are, in the main, the preoccupation of women. Scholars have been, in general, content to catalogue Margery Kempe as a rather inferior mediaeval mystic, overlooking her major contributions to the emancipation of women. Not until this reappraisal has it seemed justifiable to apply the term feminist to Margery Kempe.

Although historical documents indicate that both women came from a merchant background, their dissimilarities cannot be explained simply by the centuries that separate them. We have seen that the rising bourgeoisie from the fifteenth century onwards was conscious of the importance of learning, yet shrewd Margery Kempe remained the self-declared illiterate who apparently needed to experience the conventional deprivations of a mediaeval mother and wife, had to touch rock-bottom, before she could summon the strength to break free and define the course of her own life. Outstandingly intelligent Mary Astell, on the other hand, became the sophisticated lady whose feminist works exposed lack of education as a major cause of the deplorable situation of women. Furthermore, she declared spinsters an asset rather than a burden to society. Her discontent at the lot of women and her readiness to identify with actual predicaments must have driven her to find a room of her own, in Virginia Woolf's sense. Once ensconced and living according to her theory in an exclusive circle of women, Mary Astell was free to write.

Where Margery Kempe ultimately achieved at-onement by fulfilling her wishes within a fifteenth century social framework, Mary Astell's attempt at incorporating new ideas into the existing system failed. The author of *A Serious Propopsal* realized that the times were not ready for her innovations. Rather than pursue a futile dream, she moved on to apply her energies in areas where she saw possibilities for success.

In her campaign for women to be accepted as responsible members of society, Mary Astell fought discrimination on grounds of gender or marital status. Having forged individual freedom within marriage, Margery Kempe had already to some extent put into practice what Mary Astell was later to advocate.

Neither pursued equal rights in the twentieth century meaning of the word, or attempted to overturn the existing social system. However, both fought for a sphere where they could make their own decisions. The author of the *Serious Proposal*, having identified the obstacles and presented concrete solutions, ceased to fight for all women once her suggestion had been dismissed. In her own lifestyle, she gave substance to her theory by continuing to support herself. When she had exhausted the usefulness of writing about women, she did not stop publishing, but moved to subjects she knew would attract readers.

In contrast, the mediaeval housewife, with intuitive fluidity, eased her way from the hurly burly of living her life to the relative tranquility of widowhood in which she could create her *Book*. Throughout her life she had had neither the time nor, presumably, the inclination to write. As I have suggested, once she had stopped travelling and did dictate her autobiography, she engaged in erecting a monument to her existence rather than conscious teaching. Mary Astell, on the other hand, was at all times a professional educator.

Far from showing any contempt for men, Margery Kempe liked them. She stayed in marriage and adapted it to suit her. Moreover, she 'created' her new partner, Jesus, in the form of a beautiful man. While Mary Astell was happy to live in a society of women only, one might conjecture that Margery Kempe would have been extremely unhappy in a community without men. On her own admission, she remained loyal to her husband, remembering "how sche in hir 30ng age had ful many delectabyl thowtys, ... & inordinat louys to hys persone" (*Book*, chap 76). Focussing on women not men, Mary Astell strove to maintain calm dignity. As has been pointed out, the only time she deviated was when she attacked men's unfairness to women. Mary Astell was, to use a twentieth century term, a sexist however moderate; Margery Kempe most certainly was not.

The most striking aspect of a comparison is that two such different characters could come to the same definition of independence. Their desire for chastity is the ultimate concretion of a defined sphere of their own. However, where in Mary Astell's case the application of logical thinking led first to a careful plan and ultimately to the abandonment of her design, Margery Kempe, virtually thanks to the absence of any overall cognitive process, was able to narrow the focus on to her goal, selecting only those events she was able to process and use to the advantage of a development that led to her independence.

Three hundred years before Mary Astell, "The First Feminist", proposed means to greater liberty and exhorted more self-esteem in women, Margery Kempe had, through her own lifestyle, demonstrated freedom achieved. Too much has been made of her defamatory use of "*p*ys creatur". The very existence of the *Book* proves that she assessed herself as a woman worth writing about.

Three hundred years after Mary Astell, when some education has become compulsory for all girls, at least in the western world, and women are expected to use their freedom of choice, in marriage and elsewhere, we can still look back to Margery Kempe with amazement. Most of what Mary Astell advocated has been won. Margery Kempe, however, not only defined problems experienced in marriage, she managed to solve issues which are still under debate in the last decade of our century.

X BIBLIOGRAPHY

For a complete list of published texts written by women in England before 1700 the reader is referred to Hilda Smith's and Claudia Cardinale's *Women and Literature of the Seventeenth Century*, and Patricia Crawford's "Provisional Checklist of Women's Published Writings 1600-1700" in *Women in English Society*. Ed. Mary Prior. op. cit., pp 234-262.
Texts written by women before 1600 are included in the present bibliography.

a) Primary Sources

Anger, Jane. *Jane Anger her protection for women. To defend them against the Scandalous Reports of a Late Surfeiting Lover and all other like Venerians that complain to be overcloyed with women's kindness.* London:1589.

Astell, Mary. *Letters Concerning the Love of God.* London: 1693.

Astell, Mary. *A Serious Proposal to the Ladies.* Part I. London: 1696.

Astell, Mary. *A Serious Proposal to the Ladies.* Part II. London: 1697.

Astell, Mary. *Some Reflections Upon Marriage.* London: 1700.

The Correspondence of Anne, Viscountess Conway, Henry More and Their Friends 1642-1684. Ed. Margery Hope Nicolson. New Haven: Yale University Press, 1930.

Lady Lettice Vi-Countess Falkland Ed. and intro. M.F. Howard. London: John Murray, 1908.

Ellinor Fettiplace's Receipt Book. 1604 Ed. Hilary Spurling. London: Penguin, 1986.

Fiennes, Celia. *Travel Journals.* 1685-1703. Ed. C. Morris. op. cit.

Hoby, Lady Margaret. *The Diary of Lady Mary Hoby.* Ed. D.M. Meads. Boston MA: George Routledge, 1930.

Julian of Norwich. *A Book of Showings to the Anchoress Julian of Norwich.* Eds. Edmund Colledge and James Walsh. 2 vols. Toronto: Pontifical Institute of Mediaeval Studies, 1978.

Julian of Norwich. *Revelations of Divine Love.* Trans. Clifton Wolters. Harmondsworth: Penguin Books, 1966.

Kempe, Margery. *The Book of Margery Kempe.* Ed. Sanford Brown Meech, Prefatory Note by Hope Emily Allen. Oxford: Oxford University Press, 1982.

Kempe, Margery. *The Book of Margery Kempe.* Trans. Barry Windeatt. London: Penguin Books, 1985.

Makin, Bathsua. *Essay to Revive the Antient Education of Gentlewomen.* (1673)

Montagu, Lady Mary Wortley. *Letters and Works.* Ed. Lord Wharncliffe. N.p., 1837.

Paston Letters and Papers of the Sixteenth Century. Ed. Norman Davies. Oxford: Clarendon, 1971.

The Paston Letters 1422-1509. Ed. James Gairdner. London: Constable, 1900.

The Correspondence of Lady Katharine Paston 1603-27. Ed. Ruth Hughey Norfolk Record Society XIV, 1941.

Van Schurman, Anna Maria. *The Learned Maid or, whether a Maid may be a Scholar.* 1659

Thornton, Alice. *"The Autobiography of Mrs. Alice Thornton"* (1627-1707) Ed. C. Jackson
Surtees Society LXII, 1875.

Tyler, Margaret, Trans. *The Mirrour of princely Deedes and Knyghthood* by Diego Ortuñez de Calahorra. 1578. "Epistle to the Reader".

The Letters of Rachel Wriothesley, Lady Russell. From the manuscript at Woburn Abbey with an introduction vindicating the character of Lord Russell against Sir John Dalrymple etc. and the trial of William Russell for High Treason. Ed. Lord John Russell. London: J. Dove, 1826.

The Letters of Rachel Lady Russell. (London: Longman, 1853)

b) Secondary Sources and Background Reading

Abbot, H. Porter. *Diary Fiction. Writing as Action.* Ithaca and London: Cornell University Press, 1984.

Adburgham, Alison. *Women in Print: Writing Women and Women's Magazines from the Restoration to the Accession of Victoria.* London: Allen & Unwin, 1972.

Aers, David, ed. *Medieval Literature.* Brighton, Sussex: Harvester Press, 1986.

Aers, David. *Community, Gender, and Individual Identity.* English writing 1360-1430. London & New York: Routledge, 1988.

Ahrens, Rüdiger, ed. *Englische literaturkritische Essays 2. 19. und 20. Jahrhundert.* Heidelberg: Quelle und Meyer, 1975.

Aiken, William A. *Conflict in Stuart England.* Hamden CT: Archon, 1970.

Allchin, A.M. "Julian of Norwich and the Continuity of Tradition". *The Medieval Mystical Tradition in England.* Papers read at The Exeter Symposium, July 1980. Ed. Marion Glasscoe. op. cit. pp 72-85.

Allen, Hope Emily. "Prefatory Note" (pp liii-lxviii), "Notes and Appendices" (pp 255-350) to *The Book of Margery Kempe.* op. cit.

Anderson, Rev. James. *Memorable Women of Puritan Times.* London: 1862.

Andersen, Margret. "Feminism as a Criterion of the Literary Critic." *Feminist Literary Criticism. Essays on Theory,*

Poetry and Prose. Eds. Brown, Cheryl C. and Karen Olson. op. cit. pp 1-11.

Anon. "Women Writers among Friends of the Seventeenth Century and Later." *Journal of Friends Historical Society* 10 (1921): pp 93-96.

Atkinson, Clarissa. *Mystic and Pilgrim. The "Book" and the World of Margery Kempe*. Ithaca NY: Cornell University Press, 1983.

Baker, Derek, ed. *Medieval Women*. Oxford: Basil Blackwell, 1978.

Ballard, George. *Memoirs of Several Ladies of Great Britain*. 1752.

Beckwith, Sarah. "A Very Material Mysticism: The Medieval Mysticism of Margery Kempe." *Medieval Literature*. Ed. David Aers, op. cit. pp 34-58.

Beer, Frances. *Women and Mystical Experience in the Middle Ages*. Woodbridge: The Boydell Press, 1992.

Beer, Frances. *Julian of Norwich: Revelations of Divine Love*. Heidelberg: Winter, 1978.

Beilin, Elaine V. Women Writers of the Renaissance. Princeton NJ: Princeton University Press, 1987

Bennett, Henry S. *Six Medieval Men and Women*. Cambridge: Cambridge University Press, 1955.

Bennett, Henry S. *The Pastons and Their England*. Cambridge: Cambridge University Press, 1970.

Benstock, Shari, ed. *Feminist Issues in Literary Scholarship.* Bloomington and Indianapolis: Indiana University Press, 1987.

Bernbaum, Ernest. "Mrs. Behn's Biography. A Fiction." *PLMA* 38,3 (1913): pp 432-453.

Best, Mary Agnes. *Rebel Saints.* 1925. Freeport NY: Books for Libraries Press, 1968.

Blain, Virginia, Patricia Clements, and Isobel Grundy eds. *The Feminist Companion to Literature in English.* London: B.T. Batsford, 1990.

Blodgett, Harriet. *Centuries of Female Days.* Englishwomen's private diaries. Gloucester: Sutton, 1989.

Blodgett, Harriet. *Capacious Hold-All.* An Anthology of Englishwomen's Diary Writings. Charlottesville: University Press of Virginia, 1991.

Boitani, Piero, and Anna Torti, eds., *Genres, Themes, and Images in English Literature.* The J.A.W. Bennett Memorial Lectures, Perugia. Tübingen: Gunter Narr, 1986.

Boitani, Piero, and Anna Torti, eds. *Religion in the Poetry and Drama of the Late Middle Ages in England.* Cambridge: D.S. Brewer,1990.

Bottrall, Margaret. *Every Man a Phoenix. Studies in Seventeenth Century Autobiography.* London: John Murray, 1958.

Boulding, Elise. *The Underside of History: A View of Women Through Time.* Boulder CO: Westview, 1976.

Bradley, Ritamary. "Julian of Norwich: Writer and Mystic." *Introduction to the Medieval Mystics of Europe.* Ed. Paul Szarmach. op.cit. pp 195-216.

Bradley, Ritamary. "The Speculum Image in Medieval Mystical Writers." *The Medieval Mystical Tradition in England.* Papers read at Dartington Hall, July 1984. Ed. Marion Glasscoe. op. cit. pp 9-27.

Bradley, Ritamary. "Perceptions of Self in Julian of Norwich's Showings." *Downside Review* 105 (1986): pp 227-239.

Brailsford, Mabel. *Quaker Women 1650-1690.* London: N.P. 1895.

Braithewaite, William C., *The Beginnings of Quakerism.* London: Macmillan & Co, 1923.

Brant, Clare and Diane Purkiss, eds., *Women, Texts and Histories 1575-1760.* London: Routledge, 1992.

Bridenthal, Renate, and Claudia Koontz, eds. *Becoming Visible.* Women in European History. New York: Houghton and Mifflin, 1977.

Brown, Cheryl C., and Karen Olson, eds. *Feminist Literary Criticism. Essays on Theory, Poetry, and Prose.* Metuchen NJ and London: Scarecrow Press, 1978.

Bruss, Elizabeth. *Autobiographical Acts. The Changing Situation of a Literary Genre.* Baltimore: Johns Hopkins University Press, 1976.

Brustein, Robert. "The Monstruous Regiment of Women." *Renaissance and Modern Essays.* Ed. Hibbard, George R. op. cit. pp 35-50.

Burrage, Champlin. *The Early English Dissenters in the Light of Recent Research 1550-1641.* Cambridge: Cambridge University Press, 1912.

Bush, Douglas. "English Literature in the Earlier Seventeenth Century." *Oxford History of English* V, Oxford: Clarendon Press, 1945.

Busshardt, Helen Marie. "Christ as Feminine in Julian of Norwich in the Light of the Psychology of C.G. Jung." Diss. Fordham University, 1985.

Bynum Walker, Caroline. *Jesus as Mother: Studies in the Spirituality of the High Middle Ages.* Berkeley: University of California Press, 1982.

Bynum Walker, Caroline, ed. *Gender and Religion: of the Complexity of Symbols.* Boston MA: Beacon Press, 1986.

Capp, B. S., *Astrology and the Popular Press.* London: Faber and Faber, 1979.

Caroll, Berenice A. *Liberating Women's History: Theoretical and Critical Essays.* Urbana: University of Illinois Press, 1976.

Charlton, Kenneth. *Education in Renaissance England.* London: Routledge and Kegan Paul, 1965.

Cholmeley, Katharine, *Margery Kempe: Genius and Mystic.* London: Longman and Green, 1947.

Clifford, James L. *Biography as an Art.* Selected Criticism 1560-1960. London: Oxford University Press, 1962.

Clark, Alice. *Working Life of Women in the Seventeenth Century.* 1911. London: Routledge & Kegan Paul, 1982.

Clark, Rev. J.P.H. "Nature, Grace and the Trinity in Julian of Norwich. *Downside Review* 340 (1982): pp 203-220.

Clark, Rev. J.P.H. "Predestination of Christ According to Julian of Norwich." *Downside Review* 339 (1982): pp 79-91.

Colledge, Eric. *The Mediaeval Mystics of England.* London: John Murray, 1962.

Collier-Bendelow, Margaret. *Gott ist unsere Mutter.* Freiburg: Frauenforum Herder, 1989.

Collis, Louise. *The Apprentice Saint.* London: Michael Joseph, 1964.

Coontz, Stephanie, and Peta Henderson, eds. *Women's Work, Men's Property.* London: Verso, 1968.

Cooper, Austin. *Julian of Norwich. Reflections on Selected Texts.* Wellwood: Burn & Oates, 1987.

Copeland, Rita. "Richard Rolle and the Rhetorical Theory of the Levels of Style". *The Medieval Mystical Tradition in England.* Papers read at Dartington Hall, July 1984. Ed. Marion Glasscoe. op. cit. pp 55-80.

Corcoran, Marlena G. *The Foresaid Creature. The Construction of the Subject in the Book of Margery Kempe.* unpubl. paper, 1988.

Coventry, Patmore. *The Rod, the Root and the Flower.* 1907. Salem MA: Ayer, 1950.

Coward, Rosalind. "This novel changes lives. are women's novels feminist novels?" *Feminist Review* 5 (1980): pp 53-64.

Crawford, Patricia. "Women's Published Writings 1600-1700." *Women in English Society 1500-1800.* Ed. Mary Prior. op. cit. pp 211 - 232.

Crawford, Patricia. "From the Woman's View. Pre-industrial England 1500-1700." 1983. *Exploring Woman's Past.* Ed. Patricia Crawford, op. cit. pp 49-86.

Crawford, Patricia, ed. *Exploring Women's Past.* London: Allen & Unwin, 1984.

Cross, Claire. " 'Great Reasoners in Scripture': The Activities of Women Lollards 1380-1530." *Medieval Women.* Ed. Derek Baker, op. cit. pp 359-380.

Cuddon, J.A. *A Dictionary of Literary Terms.* 1977. London: Penguin, 1979.

Datsko Barker, Paula S. "The Motherhood of God in Julian of Norwich's Theory." *Downside Review* 341 (1982): pp 290-304.

Davies, Norman. *Paston Letters and Papers of the Sixteenth Century.* Oxford: Clarendon, 1971.

Day, Robert Adams. *Told in Letters. Epistolary Fiction Before Richardson.* Ann Arbor: University of Michigan Press, 1966.

Dehler, Kathleen. "The Need to Tell it All: A Comparison of Historical and Modern 'Confessional' Writing." *Feminist Literary Criticism. Essays on Theory, Poetry and Prose.* Eds. Cheryl C. Brown and Karen Olson. op. cit. pp 339-353.

Delaney, Paul. *British Autobiography in the Seventeenth Century.* London: Routledge and Kegan Paul, 1969.

Delaney, Sheila. *Writing Woman: Women Writers and Women in Literature, Medieval to Modern.* New York: Schocken Books, 1983.

Delaney, Sheila. "Sexual Economics in Chaucer's Wife of Bath and the Book of Margery Kempe." *Minnesota Review* 5 (1975): pp 105-115.

D.H.S., a Benedictine of Stanbrook. "English Spiritual Writers. Dame Julian of Norwich" *Clergy Review* 44 (1959): pp 705-720

Dickman, Susan. "Margery Kempe and the English Devotional Tradition." *The Medieval Mystical Tradition in England.* Papers read at Dartington Hall, July 1984. Ed. Marion Glasscoe. op. cit. pp 156-172.

Dickman, Susan. "Margery Kempe and the Continental Tradition of the Pious Woman." *Medieval Mystical Tradition in England.* Papers read at Dartington Hall, July 1984. Ed. Marion Glasscoe. op. cit. pp 150-168.

Donnison, Jean. *Midwives and Medical Men. A History of Inter-Professional Rivalries and Women's Rights.* London and New York: Heinemann Educational Books, 1977.

Dudek, Louis. *Literature and the Press.* Toronto: Ryerson Press, 1962.

Dudek, Louis. *The First Person in Literature.* Toronto: CBC Publications, 1967.

Dronke, Peter. *Women Writers of the Middle Ages.* Cambridge: Cambridge University Press, 1984.

Eakin, Paul John. *Fictions in Autobiography. Studies in the Art of Self-Invention.* Princeton NJ: Princeton University Press, 1985.

Ebner, Dean. *Autobiography in Seventeenth Century England. Theology and the Self.* Den Haag, Paris: Mouton, 1971.

Edel, Leon. *Literary Biography (Writing Lives).* New York: Norton, 1984.

Edkins, Carol. "Quest for Community: Spiritual Autobiographies of Eighteenth Century Quaker and Puritan Women in America." *Women's Autobiography. Essays in Criticism.* Ed. Estelle C. Jelinek. op. cit. pp 39-52.

Edwards, Anthony S.G. ed. *Middle English Prose. A Critical Guide to Major Authors and Genres.* New Brunswick NJ: Rutgers University Press, 1986.

Egan, Susanna. *Patterns of Experience in Autobiography.* Chapel Hill and London: University of North Carolina Press, 1984.

Ellis, Deborah S. "Margery Kempe and the Hot Caudle." *Essays in Art and Sciences* 14 (1985): pp 1-11.

Ellis, Deborah S. "The Merchant's Wife's Tale: Language, sex, and commerce in Margery Kempe and Chaucer." *Exemplaria* 2 (1990): pp 595-626.

Elton, Geoffrey R. *Reform and Reformation in England 1509-1558.* Cambridge MA: Harvard University Press, 1977.

Engler, Balz, ed. *Writing and Culture*. SPELL, Swiss Papers in English Language and Literature. Tübingen: Gunter Narr, 1992.

Evelyn, John. *The Life of Mrs Godolphin*. London: Oxford University Press, 1939.

Feder, Lillian. *Madness in Literature*. Princeton N.J.: Princeton University Press, 1980.

Ferguson, Moira, ed. *First Feminists. British Women Writers 1578-1799*. Indiana: Indiana University Press, 1985.

Fienberg, Nona. "Thematics of Value in *The Book of Margery Kempe*." *MP* 89 (1989): pp 132-141.

Figes, Eva. *Sex and Subterfuge. Women Novelists to 1850*. London: Macmillan & Co., 1982.

Figes, Eva. *The Seven Ages*. New York: Pantheon, 1986.

Fisher, Joan. *The Creative Art of Needlepoint Tapestry*. London: Hamlyn, 1972.

Foss, David R. "From God as Mother to Priest as Mother: Julian of Norwich and the Movement for the Ordination of Women." *Downside Review* 357(1986): pp 214-226.

Fothergill, Robert A. *Private Chronicles. A Study of English Diaries*. London: Oxford University Press, 1974.

Fox, Evelyn. "The Diary of an Elizabethan Gentlewoman." *Transactions of the Royal Historical Society* 3rd Series, vol II(1908).

Fraser, Antonia. *The Weaker Vessel. Woman's Lot in Seventeenth Century England*. London: Weidenfeld & Nicholson, 1984.

Fries, Maureen. "Margery Kempe." *An Introduction to the Medieval Mystics of Europe.* Ed. Paul Szarmach, op. cit., pp 217-236.

Garbàty, Thomas J. *Medieval English Literature.* Lexington, MA: Heath, 1984.

Gairdner, James ed. *The Paston Letters 1422-1509.* London: Constable, 1900.

Gartenberg, Patricia, and Nena Wittemore. "A Checklist of Women in Print 1475-1640." *Bulletin of Bibliography and Magazine Notes* 34.1 (1977): pp 1-13.

Gatta, Julia. *Three Spiritual Directors for our Time.* Cambridge MA: Cowley, 1987.

Gies, Frances and Joseph Gies. *Women in the Middle Ages.* New York: Barnes & Noble, 1978.

Gilbert, Sandra C.M., and Susan D.D. Gubar, eds. "Ceremonies of the Alphabet: Female Grandmatologies and the Female Autograph." *The Female Autograph.* Eds. Donna C. Stanton and Jeanine Parisier Plottel, op. cit. pp 23-77.

Gilbert, Sandra M, and Susan Gubar, eds. *The Norton Anthology of Literature by Women. The Tradition in English.* New York and London: W.W. Norton, 1985.

Glasscoe, Marion, ed. *The Medieval Mystical Tradition in England.* Papers read at the Exeter Symposium, July 1980. Exeter: University of Exeter, 1980.
Glasscoe, Marion, ed. *The Medieval Mystical Tradition in England.* Papers read at Dartington Hall, 1984. Cambridge: D.S. Brewer, 1984.

Gnüg, Hiltrud, and Renate Möhrmann, Hrsg. *Frauen, Literatur, Geschichte. Schreibende Frauen vom Mittelalter bis zur Gegenwart.* Stuttgart: Metzlersche Verlagsbuchhandlung, 1985.

Goodman, Anthony E. "The piety of John Brunham's daughter of Lynn." *Medieval Women.* Ed. Derek Baker, op. cit. pp 347-358.

Goodman, Kay. "Weibliche Autobiographien." 1985. *Frauen, Literatur, Geschichte.* Hrsg. Hiltrud Gnüg und Renate Möhrmann, op. cit. pp 289-300.

Goreau, Angeline. *Reconstructing Aphra.* London: Oxford University Press, 1980.

Goreau, Angeline. *The Whole Duty of a Woman: Female Writers in the Seventeenth Century.* Garden City: The Dial Press, 1985.

Goulianos, Joan, ed. *By a Woman Writt. Literature from Six Centuries by and about Women.* Indianapolis: Bobbs-Merrill, 1973.

Gray, Douglas. "Popular Religion and late Medieval English Literature." *Religion in the Poetry and Drama of the Late Middle Ages.* Eds. Boitani Piero, and Anna Torti. op. cit. pp 1-28.

Gray, Douglas, ed. and comp., *Oxford History of English Literature. Middle English Literature 1100-1400.* Oxford: Clarendon, 1990.

Gray, Douglas. "Mystical Writings: *The Cloud of Unknowing;* Hilton; Julian of Norwich." *Oxford History of English Literature. Middle English Literature 1100-1400.* 1986. Oxford: Clarendon, 1990. pp 301-334

Griffiths, Rev. R.G. "Joyce Jeffries of Ham Castle. A 17th Century Business Gentlewoman." *Transactions of the Worcestershire Archeological Society* X(1933): pp 1-35.

Griffiths, Rev. G.R. "Joyce Jeffries of Ham Castle. A 17th Century Business Gentlewoman." *Transactions of the Worcestershire Archeological Society XI(1934)*: pp 1-16.

Grundy, Isobel, and Susan Wiseman, eds. *Women, Writing, History 1640-1740.* London: B.T. Batsford, 1992.

Gunn, Janet Varner. *Autobiography: Toward a Poetics of Experience.* Philadelphia: University of Pennsylvania Press, 1982.

Gusdorf, Georges. "Conditions and Limits of Autobiography." *Essays Theoretical and Critical.* Trans. and ed. James Olney. op. cit. pp 28-48.

Hackett, Helen. " 'Yet Tell Me Some Such Fiction': Lady Mary Wroth's *Urania* and the 'Feminity' of Romance." *Women, Texts and Histories.* Eds. Clare Brant and Diane Purkiss. op. cit. pp 39-68.

Hagstrum, Jean H. *Sex and Sensibility. Ideal and Erotic Love from Milton to Mozart.* Chicago and London: The University of Chicago Press, 1980.

Haller, William. *The Rise of Puritanism.* New York: Columbia University Press, 1938.

Haller, William, and Godfrey Davies, eds. *The Leveller Tracts 1647-1653.* New York: Columbia University Press, 1944.

Harding, Wendy. "Body into Text: *'The Book of Margery Kempe'.* " *Feminist Approaches to the Body in Medieval Literature.* Eds. Linda Lomperis and Sarah Stanbury. op. cit. pp 168-188.

Harrison, G. B., ed. *The Letters of Queen Elizabeth I.* 1935. London: Cassell, 1968.

Harvey, Rev. Ralph, ed. and intro. *The Fire of Love* of Richard Rolle. London: Kegan Paul, Trench, Trübner, 1896.

Heffernan, Thomas J., ed. *The Popular Literature of Medieval England.* Knoxville: University of Tennessee Press, 1985.

Heimmel, Jennifer P. *"God is Our Mother.": Julian of Norwich and the Medieval Image of Christian Feminine Divinity.* Salzburg: Salzburg Studies in English Literature under the Direction of Professor Erwin A. Stürzl. Elizabethan and Renaissance Studies Editor: Dr. James Hogg. Salzburg: Salzburg Studies in English Literature 92:5, 1982. Insitut für Anglistik und Amerikanistik, Universität Salzburg.

Hibbard, George R., ed. *Renaissance and Modern Essays.* London: Routledge & Kegan Paul, 1966.

Higgins, Patricia. "The Reactions of Women, with Special Reference to Women Petitioners." *Politics, Religion and the English Revolution 1640-1649.* Ed. Brian Manning. op. cit. pp 179-224.

Hill, Bridget, ed. and intro. *The First English Feminist. Reflections Upon Marriage and Other Writings by Mary Astell.* Aldershot: Gower, 1986.

Hill, Christopher. *The World Turned Upside Down. Radical Ideas during the English Revolution.* Harmondsworth, Penguin Books, 1972.

Hinderer, Drew E. "On Rehabilitating Margery Kempe." *Studia Mystica* 5 (1982): pp 27-43.

Hirsh, John C. "Margery Kempe." *Middle English Prose. A Critical Guide to Major Authors and Genres.* Ed. A.S.G. Edwards. op. cit. pp 109-119.

Hirsh, John C. *The Revelations of Margery Kempe. Paramystical practices in late medieval England.* New Brunswick NJ: Rutgers University Press, 1984.

Hirsh, John C. *Hope Emily Allen.* Oklahoma: Pilgrim Books, 1988.

Hobby, Elaine. "Breaking the Silence." unpublished paper read at the Berkshire Conference of Woman Historians, Smith College MA, 1984.

Hobby, Elaine. *Virtue of Necessity. English Women's Writing 1649-88.* London: Virago, 1988.

Holbrook, Sue Ellen. "Margery Kempe and Wynkyn de Worde." *The Medieval Mystical Tradition in England.* Exeter Symposium 4. Ed. Marion Glasscoe. Cambridge: Brewer, 1987. pp 27-46.

Howarth, William L. "Some Principles of Autobiography." *Metaphors of Self: The Meaning of Autobiography.* Ed. James Olney. op. cit. pp 84-114.

Jacobus, Mary, ed. *Writing Women and Writing about Women.* London: Croom Helm, 1979.

Jacobus, Mary. "The Difference of View." *Writing Women and Writing about Women.* Ed. Mary Jacobus. op. cit. pp 10-22.

James, William. *Pragmatism.* 1907.

Janson, Henry W. *History of Art.* London: Thames and Hudson, 1986.

Jantzen, Grace M. *Julian of Norwich. Mystic and Theologian.* London: SPCK, 1987.

Jelinek, Estelle C., ed. *Women's Autobiography. Essays in Criticism.* Bloomington and London: Indiana University Press, 1980.

Jelinek, Estelle C. "Teaching Women's Autobiographies." *College English* 38(1976): pp 32-45.

Johnson, G W. *The Evolution of Woman. From Subjection to Comradeship.* London: R. Holden & Co, 1926.

Jones, Katherine. "The English Mystic Julian of Norwich." *Medieval Women Writers.* Ed. Katharina M. Wilson, op. cit. pp 269-297.

Juhasz, Susanne. "Some Deep Old Desk or Capacious Hold-All: Form and Women's Autobiography." *College English* 39 (1978): pp 663-670.

Jurgensen, Manfred, ed. *Frauenliteratur: Autorinnen, Perspektiven, Konzepte.* Bern: Lang, 1983.

Kahin, Helen Andrews. "Jane Anger and John Lyly." *PMLA* 8 (1947): pp 31-35.

Kanner, Barbara, ed. *The Women of England. From Anglo-Saxon Times to the Present.* London: Mansell, 1980.

Keller, Barbara. *Woman's Journey Toward Self and Its Literary Exploration.* Bern: Peter Lang, 1986.

Kelly-Gadol, Joan. "Did Women Have a Renaissance?" *Becoming Visible: A History of European Women.* Eds. Bridenthal, Renate and Claudia Koontz, op cit. pp175-202.

Kelso, Ruth. *Doctrine for the Lady of Renaissance.* Urbana: University of Illinois Press, 1956.

Kendall, Paul Murray. *The Art of Biography.* London: Allen & Unwin, 1965.

Kinnaird, Joan K. "Mary Astell and the Conservative Contribution to English Feminism." *Journal of British Studies* 19 (1979): pp 53-75.

Knapp, Samuel L. *Female Biography containing notices of Distinguished Women.* Philadelphia: Leary & Getz, n.d.

Knowles, David. *The English Mystical Tradition.* 1961. London: Burns & Oates, 1964.

Knowlton, Sister Mary Arthur. *The Influence of Richard Rolle and of Julian of Norwich on the Middle English Lyrics.* The Hague: Mouton, 1973.

Lagorio, Valerie M., and Ritamary Bradley. *The Fourteenth Century English Mystic. A Comprehensive Annotated Bibliography.* New York NY: Garland, 1981.

Lagorio, Valerie M. ed. *Mysticism Medieval and Modern.* Salzburg: Salzburg Studies in English Literature under the Direction of Professor Erwin A. Stürzl. Elizabethan and Renaissance Studies Ed. Dr. James Hogg 92:20. Institut für Anglistik und Amerikanistik, Universität Salzburg, 1986.

Lagorio, Valerie M. "Defensorium Contra Oblectratores." *Mysticism Medieval and Modern.* Ed. Valerie M. Lagorio. op. cit. pp 29-49.

Lederer, Wolfgang. *The Fear of Women.* New York: Grune & Stratton, 1968.

Leisi, Ernst. 1978. *Paar und Sprache.* Heidelberg: Quelle & Meyer, 1993.

Lejeune, Phillippe. "Autobiography in the Third Person." *New Literary History* 9/1(1977): pp 27-50.

Leuba, James H. *The Psychology of Religious Mysticism.* London: AMS Press, 1925.

Lewalski, Barbara Kiefer. *Writing Women in Jacobean England.* Cambridge MA: Harvard University Press, 1993.

Lewis, Clive S. *Studies in Medieval and Renaissance Literature.* Cambridge: Cambridge University Press, 1966.

Lewis, Clive S. *English Literature in the Sixteenth Century.* Oxford: Oxford University Press,1968.

Liddell, Robert. *A Treatise on the Novel.* Oxford: Alden, 1947.

Lilley, Kate. "Blazing Worlds: Seventeenth Century Women's Utopian Writing." *Women, Texts and Histories.* Eds. Clare Brant and Diane Purkiss. op. cit. pp 102-133.

Lochrie, Karma. *Margery Kempe and the Translations of the Flesh*. Philadelphia: University of Pennsylvania Press, 1992.

Lomperis, Linda, and Sarah Stanbury, eds. *Feminist Approaches to the Body in Medieval Literature*. Philadelphia: University of Pensylvania Press, 1993.

Lubbock, Percy. *The Craft of Fiction*. 1921. New York: Viking Press, 1972.

Lubin, A. "Mysticism and Creativity." *Mysticism: Quest or Psychic Disorder?* Group for the Advancement of Psychiatry 9 (1976): pp 787-798.

Lucas, Angela M. *Women in the Middle Ages. Religion, Marriage and Letters*. Brighton, Sussex: Harvester, 1983.

Lucas, Elona C. "The Enigmatic, Threatening Margery Kempe." *Downside Review* 105 (1986): pp 294-306.

Mackerness, E.D. "Margaret Tyler, an Elizabethan Feminist." *Notes and Queries* 3(1946): pp 112-113.

Madelva, Sister Maria. "Dame Julian of Norwich." *English Studies* 11 (1955): pp 21-32.

Mahl, Mary R., and Helen Koon, eds. *The Female Spectator. Women Writers before 1800*. Old Westbury, NY: Feminist Press, 1977.

Maisonneuve, Roland. *L'univers visionnaire de Julian of Norwich*. Diss. Université de Paris, 1979. Atelier national de réproductions de thèses, 1982.

Mandel, Barett J. *Full of Life Now. Essays Theoretical and Critical*. Princeton: Princeton University Press, 1980.

Manning, Brian, ed. *Politics, Religion and the English Cicvil War.* London: Edward Arnold, 1976.

Manning, Brian. *The English People and the English Revolution 1640-1649.* London: Heinemann, 1976.

Masek, Rosemary, "Women in an Age of Transition 1485-1714." *The Women of England.* Ed. Barbara Kanner. op. cit. pp 138-183.

Mason, Mary G., and Carol H. Green, eds. *Journeys: Autobiographical Writings by Women.* Boston: G.K. Hall, 1979.

Mason, Mary G. "The Other Voice. Autobiographies of Women Writers. *Autobiography: Essays Theoretical and Critical.* Ed. James Olney. op. cit. pp 207-235.

Matthews, William. *British Diaries. An Annotated Bibliography of British Diaries Written between 1442 and 1942.* Berkeley: University of California Press, 1950.

Matthews, William. *British Autobiographies.* Los Angeles: Anchor Books, 1968.

Matthews, William, and Ralph W. Rader. *Autobiography, Biography and the Novel.* Berkeley: University of California Press, 1973.

McIlquhan, Harriet. "Mary Astell, a Seventeenth Century Advocate for Women." *Westminster Review* 149 (1898): pp 440-449.

McIlquhan, Harriet. *Lady Mary Wortley Montagu and Mary Astell.* London: N.P. 1899.

McArthur, Ellen A. "Women petitioners and Parliament." *English Historical Review* XCIII(1909): pp 698-709.

McKeon, Michael. *The Origins of the English Novel 1600-1740.* Baltimore: Johns Hopkins University Press, 1987.

Meale, Carol M. *Women and Literature in Britain 1150-1500.* Cambridge: Cambridge University Press, 1993.

Mendelson, Sara. *Women in Seventeenth Century England.* Brighton, Sussex: Harvester Press, 1982.

Meyer, Dennis G. *The Scientific Lady in England 1650-1760. An Account of Her Rise with Emphasis on the Major Roles of the Telescope and Microscope.* Berkeley: University of California Press, 1955.

Meyer-Spacks, Patricia. "Reflecting Women." *Yale Review* 63 (1973): pp 26-42.

Meyer-Spacks, Patricia. *The Female Imagination.* New York: Alfred Knopf, 1975.

Meyer-Spacks, Patricia. *Imagining a Self. Autobiography and Novel in Eighteenth Century England.* Cambridge MA: Harvard University Press, 1976.

Meyer-Spacks, Patricia. "Stages of Life: Notes on Autobiography and the Life Cycle." *Boston University Journal* 25 (1977): pp 7-17.
Meyer-Spacks, Patricia. "Women's Stories, Women's Selves." *Hudson Review* 30 (1977): pp 29-46.

Mish, Charles C., ed. *Restoration Prose Fiction 1666-1700.* Lincoln: University of Nebraska Press, 1970.

Mish, Charles C. *Short Fiction of the Seventeenth Century.* New York: New York University Press, 1963.

Mitchell, Juliet. *The Longest Revolution. Essays in Feminism. Literature and Psychoanalysis.* London: Virago Press, 1984.

Mitchison, Naomi. *You May Well Ask.* London: Victor Gollancz, 1979.

Moers, Ellen. *The Great Writers. Literary Women.* Garden City NY: Anchor Books, 1977.

Moir, Esther. *The Discovery of Britain: The English Tourists 1540-1840.* London: Routledge & Kegan Paul, 1964.

Molinari, Paul, S.J. *Julian of Norwich. The Teaching of a Fourteenth Century English Mystic.* London: Longmans, Green, 1979.

Morris, Christopher, ed. *The Illustrated Journals of Celia Fiennes.* 1947. Exeter, England: Webb & Bower, 1982.

Morris, Colin. *The Discovery of the Individual, 1050-1200.* New York: Harper & Row, 1972.

Morris, John N. *Versions of the Self.* New York: Basic Books, 1966.

Mueller, Janel L. "Autobiography of a New 'Creatur'. Female Spirituality, Selfhood, and Authorship in 'The Book of Margery Kempe'." *The Female Autograph.* Eds. Donna C. Stanton and Jeanine Parisier Plottel, op. cit. pp 63-77.

Muir, Kenneth, ed. "Elizabethan and Jacobean Prose." *Pelican Book of English Prose* I. Harmondsworth: Penguin Books, 1956.

Nicolson, Harold. *The Development of English Biography.* London: Hogarth Press, 1968.

Nist, Elizabeth A. "Tattle's Well's Faire: English Women Authors of the Sixteenth Century." *College English* 46,7 (1984): pp 702-716.

von Nolcken, Christina. "Julian of Norwich." 1984. *Middle English Prose.* Ed. A.S.G. Edwards, op. cit. pp 97-108.

Norsworthy, Laura. *The Lady of the Bleeding Heart Yard. Lady Elizabeth Hatton 1578-1646.* London: John Murray, 1935.

Notestein, Wallace. *Four Worthies.* London: Jonathan Cape, 1956.

Oakley, Anne. *Subject Women.* Oxford: Robertson,1981.

O'Brien, Kate. *English Diaries and Journals.* 1947. London: Collins, 1983.

Ober, William. "Hysteria and Mysticism Reconciled." *Psychiatry and Literature* IV (1985): pp 24-40.

Olney James. *Metaphors of Self.* Princeton: Princeton University Press, 1972.

Olney, James, ed. *Autobiography: Essays Theoretical and Critical.* Princeton: Princeton University Press, 1980.

Olney, James, ed. *Studies in Autobiography.* New York, Oxford: Oxford University Press, 1988.

Orwell, George, ed. *British Pamphleteers.* London: A. Wingate, 1948.

Otten, Charlotte F., ed. *English Women's Voices, 1540-1700.* Miami: Florida International University Press, 1992.

Ourst, George R. *Preaching in Medieval England.* Cambridge: Cambridge University Press, 1926.

Panicelli, Debra Scott. "Finding God in the Memory: Julian of Norwich and the Loss of Visions." *Downside Review* 357 (1986): pp 299-317.

Parry, Edward Abbot, ed. *Letters from Dorothy Osborne to William Temple 1652-1654.* London: S.M. Dent, 1914.

Pascal, Roy. *Design and Truth in Autobiography.* London: Routledge and Kegan Paul, 1960.

Pelphrey, Brant. *Love was His Meaning. the Theology and Mysticism of Julian of Norwich.* Salzburg: Salzburg Studies in English Literature under the Direction of Professor Erwin A. Stürzl. Elizabethan and Renaissance Studies Ed. Dr. James Hogg 92:4. Institut für Anglistik und Amerikanistik, Universität Salzburg, 1982.

Penney, Norman, ed. *The First Publishers of Truth.* London: Headley Brothers, 1907.

Perry, Ruth. *The Celebrated Mary Astell. An Early English Feminist.* Chicago: University of Chicago Press, 1986.

Pinchbeck, Ivy, and Margaret Hewitt. *Children in English Society. Tudor to Eighteenth Century.* London and Toronto: Routledge & Kegan Paul, 1969.

Pomerleau, Cynthia S. "The Emergence of Women's Autobiography in England." *Women's Autobiography.* Ed. Estelle C. Jelinek. op. cit.pp 21-38.

Ponsonby, Arthur. *More English Diaries from the XVIth to the XIXth Century.* London: Methuen, 1927.

Postan, M.M., ed. *Medieval Women.* Cambridge: Cambridge University Press, 1975.

Porter, Roy. "Margery Kempe and the Meaning of Madness." *History Today* 38 (1988): pp 39-44.

Power, Eileen. "Medieval English Nunneries." *Medieval Women.* Ed. M.M. Postan. op. cit. pp 89-99.

Prior, Mary, ed. *Women in English Society 1500-1800.* London and New York: Methuen, 1985.

Provost, William. "The English Religious Enthusiast; Margery Kempe." *Mediaeval Women Writers.* Ed. Katharina Wilson. op. cit. pp 297-302.

Purkiss, Diane. "Material Girls: The Seventeenth Century Woman Debate." Eds. Brant, Clare, and Diane Purkiss. op. cit. pp

Radice, Betty, trans. and ed. *The Cloud of Unknowing and Other Works.* 1967. London: Penguin Books, 1985.
Remandin, Paul. *Quatre mystiques anglais.* Paris: Editions du Cerf, 1945.

Renza, Louis. A. "The Veto of the Imagination: A Theory in Autobiography." *Autobiography. Essays Theoretical and Critical.* Ed. J. Olney. op. cit. pp 268-295.

Reynolds, Sister Anna Maria. "Some Literary Influences on the Revelations of Julian of Norwich." *Leeds Se* 7/8 (1952): pp 18-28.

Rich, Adrienne. *Blood, Bread and Poetry.* Selected Prose 1979-1985. 1986. London: Virago, 1987.

Riehle, Wolfgang. *The Middle English Mystics.* 1977. Trans. Bernhard Standring. London: Routledge & Kegan Paul, 1981.

Riehle, Wolfgang. "Research and the Medieval English Mystics." *Genres, Themes, and Images in English Literature.* Eds. Piero Boitani and Anna Torti. op. cit. pp 141-155.

Roberts, Josephine A. *The Poems of Lady Mary Wroth.* Baton Rouge LA: Louisiana State University Press,1983.

Robertson, Elizabeth. "Medieval Medical Views of Women and Female Spirituality in 'Ancrene Wisse' and Julian of Norwich's 'Showings'." *Feminist Approaches to the Body in Medieval Literature.* Eds. Linda Lomperis and Sarah Stanbury. op. cit. pp 142-167.

Rose, Mary Beth, ed. and intro. *Women in the Middle Ages and the Renaissance. Literary and Historical Perspectives.* Syracuse: Syracuse University Press, 1986.

Rose, Mary Beth. "Seventeenth Century Women and the Art of Autobiography." *Women in the Middle Ages and the Renaissance. Literary and Historical Perspectives.* Ed. Mary Beth Rose. op. cit. pp 245-278.

Rosenberg, Marie B., and L. v. Bergstrom, eds. *Women and Society. A Critical Review of the Literature with a Selected Annotated Bibliography.* London: Gage Publications, 1975.

Ross, Isabell. *Margaret Fell.* London: Longmans, Green, 1949.

Ross, Robert C. "Oral Life, Written Text: The Genesis of the Book of Margery Kempe." *The Year Book of English Studies. Medieval Narrative.* Special Number. Modern Humanities Research Association vol 22 (1992): pp 272-237.

Rowbotham, Sheila. *Im Dunkel der Geschichte; Frauenbewegung in England vom 17. bis 20. Jahrhundert.* 1973. Uebers. Solveig Ockenfuss, Frankfurt am Main: Campus Verlag, 1980.

Rowlands, Marie B. "Recusant Women 1560-1640." *Women in English Society.* Ed. Mary Prior. op. cit. pp 149-181.

Rowse, Alfred L. *The England of Elizabeth; the Structure of Society.* London: Macmillan, 1950.

Ruether, Rosemary R., and E.C. McLaughlin, eds. *Women of Spirit.* New York: Simon & Schuster, 1979.

Ruthven, Kenneth K. *Feminist Literary Studies.* Cambridge: Cambridge University Press, 1984.

Rüttner-Cova, Sonja. *Frau Holle. Die gestürzte Göttin.* Märchen, Mythen, Matriarchat. Basel: Sphinx-Verlag, 1986.

Sachse, William L. "Pamphlet Support for Charles I." *Conflict in Stuart England.* Ed. William A. Aiken. op. cit. pp 147-168.

Sackville-West, Virginia. *Knole and the Sackvilles.* 1922. Tonbridge: Ernest Benn, 1984.

Le Saux, Françoise. " 'Hir not lettyrd': Margery Kempe and Writing." *Writing and Culture.* Ed. Balz Engler, op. cit. pp 53-68.

Sayers, Peig. *An Old Woman's Reflection.* 1962. Oxford: Oxford University Press, 1986

Schachtel, Ernest. *Metamorphosis.* 1959. New York: Da Capo Press, 1984.

Schlauch, Margaret. *Antecedents of the English Novel.* London: Oxford University Press, 1963.

Schlueter, Paul and June Schlueter, eds., *An Encyclopedia of British Women Writers.* Chicago and London: St James Press, 1988.

Schultz, Harold J. *History of England* New York: Barnes & Noble, 1980.

Shapiro, Susan C. "Feminists in Elizabethan England." *History Today* 27 (1977): pp 703-711.

Sharrock, Catherine. "De-ciphering women and de-scribing authority: The writings of Mary Astell." *Women, Writing, History.* Eds. Isobel Grundy and Susan Wiseman. op. cit. pp 109-124.

Showalter, Elaine, ed. *Women's Liberation and Literature.* New York: Harcourt Brace Jovanovich, 1971.

Showalter, Elaine. *A Literature of Their Own.* Princeton: Princeton University Press, 1977.

Showalter, Elaine. "Towards a Feminist Poetics." *Women Writing and Writing About Women.* Ed. Mary Jacobus. op. cit. pp 10-22.

Shumaker, Wayne. *English Autobiography: Its Emergence, Materials, and Forms.* Berkeley: University of California Press, 1954.

Smith, Hilda L. *Reason's Disciples: Seventeenth Century Feminists.* Urbana: University of Illinois Press, 1982.

Smith, Hilda L., and Susan Cardinale, comps. *Women and the Literature of the Seventeenth Century: An Annotated Bibliography Based on Wing's "Short-title Catalogue".* New York and Westport: Greenwood Press, 1990.

Smith, Florence Mary. *Mary Astell.* New York: Columbia University Press, 1916.

Spedding, James, ed. *The Letters and the Life of Francis Bacon.* vol I, London: Longmans, Green, Longman, and Roberts, 1861.

Spencer, Jane. *The Rise of the Woman Novelist from Aphra Behn to Jane Austen.* Oxford: Blackwell, 1986.

Spencer, Theodore. "The History of an Unfortunate Lady." *Harvard Studies and Notes in Philology and Literature* 20 (1938): pp 43-59.

Spender, Dale. *Mothers of the Novel.* London: Pandora Press, 1986.

Spender, Dale, and Lynn Spender. *Scribbling Sisters.* 1986. Norman: University of Oklahoma Press, 1987.

Spender, Stephen. "Confessions and Autobiography." *Autobiography. Essays Theoretical and Critical.* Ed. James Olney. op. cit. pp 115-122.

Spengemann, William C. *The Forms of Autobiography. Episodes in the History of a Literary Genre.* New Haven and London: Yale University Press, 1980.

Springer, Marlene, ed. *What Manner of Woman: Essays on English and American Life and Literature.* New York: New York University Press, 1977.

Spurling, Hilary. *Elinor Fettiplace's Receipt Book.* London: Penguin Books, 1986.

Stanton, Donna C., and Jeanine Parisier Plottel, eds. *The Female Autograph.* New York: New York Literary Forum, 1984.

Stanton, Donna C. "Autogynography: Is the Subject Different?" *The Female Autograph.* Eds. Donna Stanton and Jeanine Parisier Plottel. op. cit. pp 5-22.

Stargardt, Ute. "The Beguines of Belgium and the Dominican Nuns of Germany and Margery Kempe." *The Popular Literature of Medieval England.* Ed. Th. Heffernan. op. cit. pp 277-313.

Starobinski, Jean. "The Style of Autobiography." *Autobiography. Essays Theoretical and Critical.* Ed. J. Olney. op. cit. pp 73-83.

Stone, Robert K. *Middle English Prose Style: Margery Kempe and Julian of Norwich.* The Hague: Mouton, 1970.

Stone, Lawrence. *The Family, Sex and Marriage in England 1500-1800.* London: Weidenfeld & Nicolson, 1977.

Strickland, Agnes. *Lives of the Queens of Scotland and English Princesses Connected with the Succession of Great Britain.* London: Blackwood, 1850/51.

Strickland, Agnes. *Lives of the Tudor and Stuart Princesses.* London: G. Bell, 1888.

Stuard, Susan Mosher, ed. and intro. *Women in Medieval Society.* Philadelphia: University of Pennsylvania Press, 1976.

Szarmach, Paul. *Introduction to the Medieval Mystics of Europe.* Albany: The State University of New York Press, 1984.

Thomas, Keith. "Women and the Civil War Sects." *Past and Present* 13 (1958): pp 42-57.

Thouless, Robert H. *The Lady Julian.* London: Society for Promoting Christian Knowledge, 1924.

Todd, Janet, ed. *A Dictionary of British and American Woman Writers 1660-1800.* London: Methuen, 1984.

Todd, Janet, ed., *A Dictionary of British Women Writers.* London: Routledge, 1989.

Travitsky, Betty, comp. and ed. *The Paradise of Women. Writings by English Women of the Renaissance.* Westport: Greenwood Press, 1981.

Trevelyan, George M. *Illustrated English History.* 1949. London: The Reprint Society, 1963.

Underhill, Evelyn. *Mysticism. A Study in the Nature and Development of Man's Spiritual Consciousness.* 1911. London: Methuen, 1960.

Usher Henderson, Katherine, and Barbara F. McManus. *Half Humankind. Contexts and Texts of the Controversy about Women in England 1540-1640*. Urbana and Chicago: University of Illinois Press, 1985.

Utley, Francis Lee. *The Crooked Rib. An Annotated Index to the Argument about Women in English and Scots Literature to the End of the Year 1568.* Columbus Ohio: Ohio State University Press, 1944.

Vinje, Patricia Mary. *An Understanding of Love According to Julian of Norwich.* Salzburg Studies in English Literature under the Direction of Professor Erwin A. Stürzl. Elizabethan and Renaissance Studies Editor: Dr. James Hogg 92:8. Institut für Anglistik und Amerikanistik, Universität Salzburg, 1983.

Wacker, Marie Theres, ed. *Der Gott der Männer und der Frauen.* Düsseldorf: Patmos, 1987.

Wallace, David. "Mystics and Followers in Siena and East Anglia: A Study in Taxonomy, Class and Cultural Meditation." *The Medieval Mystical Tradition in England*. Papers read at Dartington Hall, July 1984. Ed. Marion Glasscoe. op. cit. pp 169-191.

Watkin, Edward I. "In Defence of Margery Kempe." *Downside Review* 59 (1941): pp 243-263.

Watkins, Owen C. *The Puritan Experience.* London: Routledge and Kegan Paul, 1972.

Weinstein, Minna F. "Queen's Power: The Case of Katherine Parr." *History Today* 26(1976): pp 788-795.

Weintraub, Karl J. *The Value of the Individual: Self and Circumstance in Autobiography.* Chicago: University of Chicago Press, 1978.

Wiehaus, Ulrike. "Gott als Mutter in mittelalterlicher Spiritualität." *Der Gott der Männer und der Frauen.* Ed. Marie Theres Wacker. op. cit. pp 93-100.

Williams, Ethyn Morgan. "Women Preachers in the Civil War." *Journal of Modern History* (1929): pp 561-569.

Wilson, Katharina M., ed. *Medieval Women Writers.* Athens GA: University of Georgia Press, 1984.

Wilson, Katharina M., ed. *Women Writers of the Renaissance and Reformation.* Athens GA: University of Georgia Press, 1987.

Windeatt, Barry M., "The Art of Mystical Loving: Julian of Norwich." *The Medieval Mystical Tradition in England.* Papers read at The Exeter Symposium, July 1980. Ed. Marion Glasscoe. op. cit. pp 55-71.

Wolfe, Don Marion. *Leveller Manifestoes of the Puritan Revolution.* New York: T. Nelson, 1944.

Wolters, Clifton, ed. *Revelations of Divine Love.* Harmondsworth: Penguin, 1966.

Woodbridge, Linda. *Women and the English Renaissance. Literature and the Nature of Womankind 1540-1620.* Brighton, Sussex: Harvester Press, 1984.

Woodtli, Susanna. *Gleichberechtigung.* 1975. Frauenfeld: Huber, 1983.

Woolf, Virginia. *A Room of One's Own.* 1929. London: Grafton, 1987.

Wright, Luella. *The Literary Life of the Early Friends.* New York: Columbia University Press, 1932.

Wright, Luella. "Literature and Education in Early Quakerism." *University of Iowa Studies* vol. V, no 2 (1933)

Zipes, Jack, ed. *Don't Bet on the Prince. Contemporary Feminist Fairy Tales in North America and England.* Aldershot: Gower, 1986.

CHRIST CHURCH CATHEDRAL
BRIGID'S PLACE
1117 TEXAS AVE.
HOUSTON, TX 77002